THE ORDERS OF ARCHITECTURE

THE DORIC ORDER OF THE PARTHENON, ATHENS

From a Water-Colour Sketch by Lewis Vulliamy, cir. 1818, *in the possession of the Author*

THE ORDERS OF ARCHITECTURE

GREEK ROMAN AND RENAISSANCE WITH SELECTED EXAMPLES OF THEIR APPLICATION · SHOWN ON 80 PLATES ·

BY

ARTHUR STRATTON

ARCHITECT

Fellow of the Society of Antiquaries: Fellow of the Royal Institute of British Architects: Formerly Reader in Architecture in the University of London: Author of "Elements of Form and Design in Classic Architecture", "The English Interior," Etc.

WITH AN INTRODUCTION BY

A. TRYSTAN EDWARDS, M·A·

Associate of the Royal Institute of British Architects: Associate of the Town Planning Institute: Author of "Things which are Seen", etc.

STUDIO EDITIONS

LONDON

Originally Published by B T Batsford Limited 1931

This edition published 1986 by Studio Editions,
a division of Bestseller Publications Ltd,
Princess House, 50 Eastcastle Street,
London W1N 7AP.

ISBN 1 85170 071 4

Printed and bound in Great Britain by
R. J. Acford, Chichester, Sussex.

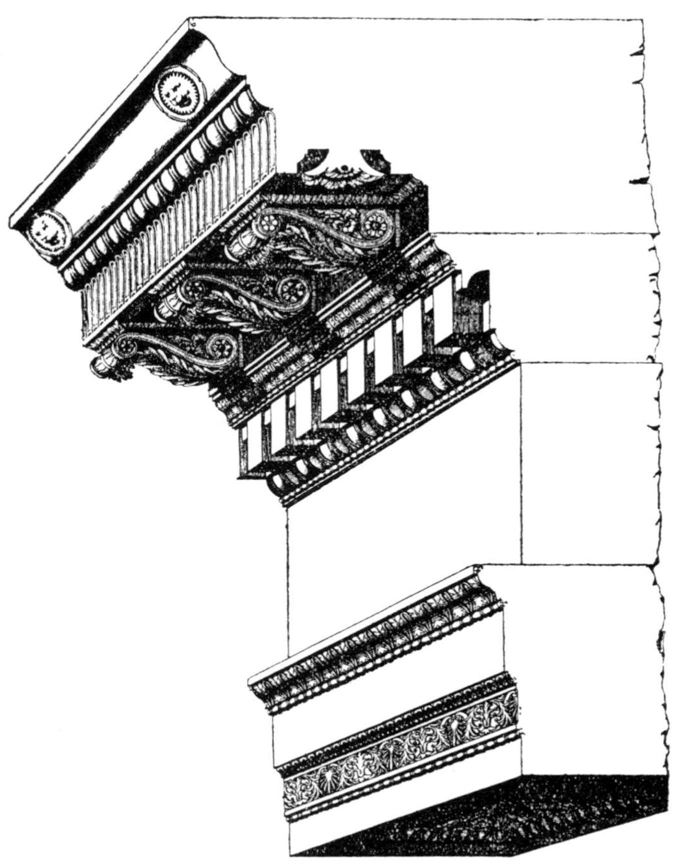

PERSPECTIVE DRAWING OF A CORINTHIAN ENTABLATURE
From an Engraving by Antonio Labacco, 1557

PREFACE AND NOTE OF ACKNOWLEDGMENT

LONG experience of teaching the Orders to students of Architecture has convinced me that a most interesting subject tends to become irksome because of its dull presentation in most of the existing books. That large numbers have been issued over a long period of time, and in many countries, does not rule out the advisability of yet another, for nearly all the specialised books of Plates show the Orders as archæological fragments, faultlessly delineated in pure line, but to the student, meaningless and lifeless in their isolation. Too long has the task of the teacher been unnecessarily difficult.

All through Classic and Renaissance times, the Orders formed an integral part of structures great and small, and this work endeavours to present them as vital elements in the design and composition of buildings, rather than as stereotyped dispositions of columns and their entablatures. If it is used in conjunction with my companion volume, " Elements of Form and Design in Classic Architecture," the student will be equipped with a working knowledge, not only of some of the best ancient and Renaissance Orders, but also of many of the best examples of their legitimate use.

The student does not readily visualise three dimensional members as they appear to the eye in solid materials without the aid of perspective, for cast shadows convey little more than the relative projections of one plane to another. Interest is quickly aroused by perspective sketches of the Orders ; many are included in the following series of Plates, and for the first time in any book on the Orders published in this country, all the scale drawings of Vignola's models are supplemented by perspective sketches.

The architects of the Renaissance systematically pursued the transformation of peristylar architecture into forms more suited to modern requirements, and canons of proportion drawn up by Vignola and published in 1563 were the first of a long series. Such a proceeding, though it doubtless safeguarded the employment of the Orders from many excesses, must be considered on the other hand to have placed them in an entirely false position, since they were handled with freedom by the Greeks and to some extent also by the Romans. Notwithstanding these canons, the Italian Renaissance presents instances that show considerable latitude in the use of accepted classic forms. The purpose which is so strongly marked in every structural and decorative member of their studied relation to one another, if rightly interpreted, promotes freedom rather than restraint. The Orders are not the stereotyped records of past ages : fashions in design change perpetually, and there is a tendency to dispense with the Orders in present-day building, but they are never likely to be discarded for any length of time by any enlightened building people, and they cannot be ignored in the curriculum of the School of Architecture.

To deal with every aspect of such a many-sided and vital subject within the confines of a single handy volume is impossible, but it is hoped that this attempt to analyse well-known forms from a present-day point of view may help to rekindle an intelligent interest in a subject which is as indispensable to the practising architect and the student to-day as it has ever been in the past. Such a collection of Plates as is here presented gains additional value by the inclusion of Italian, French, English, and American-Colonial examples.

The book is strengthened by the thoughtful and scholarly Introduction contributed by Mr A. Trystan Edwards, M.A.(Oxon), A.R.I.B.A. It has further had the advantage of helpful criticism by Mr Ronald P. Jones, M.A.(Oxon), F.R.I.B.A., and careful research by Miss Norah Davenport. The books consulted are too numerous to name. The drawings have been especially made, and without the advice of Mr Hector Corfiato, S.A.D.G., it is unlikely they would have attained such a standard. To Mr D. Hottinger I am indebted for the rendered and line originals from which the majority of the Plates have been reproduced. The frontispiece and one other Plate are from treasured originals in my possession, by Lewis Vulliamy, and amongst those who have lent measured drawings are Mr Robert S. Weir and several of my old students, whose reward will be to know that they will assist in inspiring future generations of students to appreciate buildings to which the Orders give distinction. I also thank the Council of the Royal Institute of British Architects for permission to reproduce some subjects from a collection of original Classic Drawings in the R.I.B.A. Library; Mr James Cromar Watt for Fig. vi. on Plate xiii. from his "Examples of Greek and Pompeian Decorative Work"; and Messieurs Ch. Massin et Cie, of Paris, for permission to include Figs. i.-v. on Plate xiii. and Plate xxiv., which are taken from the fine series of restorations entitled "Fragments d'Architecture Antique," edited by H. D'Espouy. Once more I have been fortunate in my Publishers, and I have found in Mr Harry Batsford, Hon. A.R.I.B.A., a keen and sympathetic co-operator who has placed his resources at my disposal that the book may be worthily launched upon the stormy waters of the architectural world.

ARTHUR STRATTON.

"Stonecot,"
Pulborough, Sussex,
May 1931.

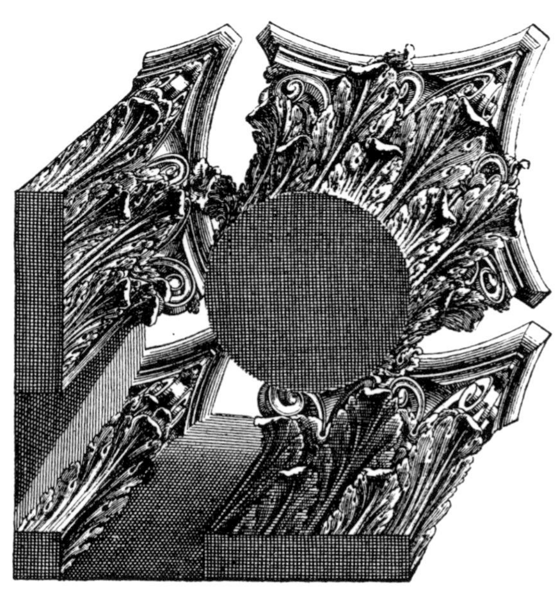

CONTENTS

THE MODULE

Several methods have been used for determining the scale of equal parts by which the Orders are measured for purposes of delineation, but they are all founded on the diameter of the column at the bottom of the shaft. It has been found convenient to take the lowest semi-diameter of the column as a unit—known as the Module—and to divide it into a given number of equal parts or minutes, the number of parts varying with the character of the Order.

In the case of the Greek and Roman Orders, the Module is universally divided into thirty parts, and this has been found to give satisfactory results. With the Italian Orders of Vignola and other Renaissance masters, however, the Module has been invariably divided into twelve parts for the Tuscan and Doric Orders, and into eighteen parts for the Ionic, Corinthian, and Composite Orders. It has been felt advisable not to depart from this long-established arrangement, as in practice considerable difficulty would arise from dividing the Module into the same number of equal parts for all the Orders. This is obvious when consideration is given to the difference in character between the detail of the sturdy Tuscan and Doric Orders and that inherent to the *finesse* of the three more graceful Orders which requires the Module to be divided into a greater number of parts than twelve if minute fractions of parts are to be avoided. For convenience, large-scale details of the Orders are best drawn with a Module divided, as in the case of the Classic Orders, into thirty parts ; this procedure has been adopted in the following Plates.

CORINTHIAN CAPITAL FROM THE BATHS AT NÎMES

THE ORDERS OF ARCHITECTURE

CHAPTER I

INTRODUCTION

No form or element of art has achieved renown comparable to that of the Classic Order, and none bears so unmistakably the imprint of genius. The Classic Order is the Classic style itself; it is still the most important of all the visible symbols which bear witness to the cultural unity of the nations of Europe and of those tributary nations which have sprung from European stock. In England, France and Germany, Italy and Spain, in America, Africa and Australia, whereever the white race has erected buildings of any consequence, column and entablature are found of a type which declares its affinity to those which the ancient Greeks developed. Surely this is a remarkable phenomenon, and yet in no book or treatise has it been adequately explained how it has come about that a form of building should have attained such universality and adapted itself to the architectural circumstances of so many different peoples and places.

A student of architecture cannot afford to be ignorant of the Order, nor will he, if he values his reputation as a critic, lightly speak in disparagement of it. Yet it is not easy to arrive at an understanding of such a complex element of style, and thus it has come about that the writers who have hitherto claimed to be authorities on this subject have for the most part been content to concentrate their attention upon its historical and archæological aspects to the neglect of the æsthetic. There are in existence many text-books describing the parts of the Order and illustrating the birth of the Classic style in Greece and its acceptance by the Romans, who spread it over the whole area of what was then the civilised world. It is also common knowledge that although during the early centuries of the Christian era the heritage of Greece and Rome was partly forgotten, there afterwards occurred that Revival of Learning described as the Renaissance, in which the Classic Order once more established an intellectual ascendancy, not seriously challenged until the latter half of the nineteenth century. There are several reasons why an attempt should now be made to revalue the Order. In fact, a more topical theme could scarcely be chosen, because the Order is one of the main subjects of dispute between the various architectural sects now warring with each other.

The Classic Order is attacked from two quarters, its principal critics being the Mediævalists and the Modernists. But besides its declared opponents there are two other classes of people, who, although nominally the champions of the Order, in reality damage its prestige and weaken its hold upon the respect of the present generation of architectural students. The first class comprises the incompetent designers who misuse the Order by associating it with bad composition and the worst type of commercial display; the second class are the archæologists who have hitherto been allowed to take charge of the promulgation of all doctrines and principles relating to the Order, and on account of their failure to appreciate the æsthetic aspect of the subject, have made it dry-as-dust.

It is scarcely conceivable that even in the most distant future of the human race the constructors of buildings will cease to employ column and lintol, which are, in fact, the names given to the vertical and horizontal constructional members of a building ; or that men should altogether surrender the ambition to combine these vertical and horizontal members in an æsthetic union. To say that the Classic Order achieves this latter object is almost tantamount to affirming that it deserves to be immortal. Such a statement, while true in itself, requires qualification. The Classic Order, in the forms in which it is best known, might indeed be immortal, and yet there might be parallel immortalities attaching to other forms in which the æsthetic union of post and beam had been accomplished in alternative ways. Here it is not proposed to indicate in what manner it might be possible to achieve these alternative harmonies between the structural members, for the immediate object is to analyse an æsthetic achievement already attained.

A great deal has been written concerning the difference between the Doric, the Ionic, and the Corinthian Orders ; yet very many people who can separate these in their mind without the least difficulty, would nevertheless be at a loss to indicate the æsthetic qualities common to them all. The kind of analysis which will be attempted here is not directed to the exposition of the well-worn theme of those archæologists who have discovered the dates and origins of the several types of Order, but will be concerned with an estimate of their usefulness and significance to the architect of to-day.

What is the Classic Order, it may be asked? This question can be best answered by the statement that the Order creates an organic unity between column and lintol. The very term organic seems to suggest that the qualities of the Order should be related with those which find expression in the forms of animate nature. If principles of composition can be discovered which are alike exemplified in the Order and in the shapes of animals and plants, it may be claimed that the Order possesses some of the vitality usually associated with the latter. Several such principles may here be mentioned, beginning with that of *Punctuation.* It will be observed that no branch of any tree or plant comes to an end abruptly as if it were cut off at random, but invariably has its ends modulated in some manner to express the fact that the branch or limb in question has come to a conclusion. Another principle of organic design which is expressed in all the forms of animate nature is that of *Inflection.* Everything which is inspired by the principle of life has each part so disposed that it appears to be naturally joined on to the adjacent parts and has its forms so modified that it expresses this relationship. To give an example of this peculiar sensitiveness to position the features of the human face may be cited : these could not be turned upside down and replaced in that disposition without completely disorganising the formal pattern, because each one of them is conscious that its summit is different from its base. When the body as a whole is considered it is also clear that the head differs from the feet, and a human being could not be turned upside down without assuming an attitude that is inappropriate and a cause of distress both to the person himself and to those who observe him. But a Classic column also has a head and a foot, and these differ from each other to express the differing functions of each. Turn the column upside down and it appears to scream at such an indignity. Yet there is no question that it could very well be of plain cylindrical shape and still perform its structural function adequately, as in fact many columns designed in what is called the "modernist" style are seen to do ; but these cylindrical columns are dead ; they have no knowledge of head or feet because their parts are neither punctuated nor inflected.

Quite the least intelligent way of approaching the Classic Order is to regard it as primarily a fulfilment of constructional requirements. Nearly all the traducers of the Order are guilty of this essential blunder. That the Order in its initial stages was the means of enabling posts to carry beams efficiently need not be disputed, but this elementary function might have been discharged, and among countless barbaric tribes doubtless was discharged, without there being created an architectural composition of such remarkable vigour as to be the foundation of a great style. The doctrinaires who think of architecture in terms of construction would make design too easy—in fact so easy that architects, if they accepted such a narrow interpretation of their office, would soon be compelled to go out of business and surrender the task of erecting buildings to the engineering profession.

The history of the Classic Order reveals the fact that the style it represents is to a large extent independent of the materials in which the various buildings exemplifying the style were executed. To anyone whose architectural taste has been formed by familiarity with the great mass of work constituting the Classic tradition this statement will, of course, seem a mere platitude, but as it is likely to be challenged by modern traducers of the Classic Order, it appears necessary to point out that once the æsthetic factor in design is recognised, the influence of materials upon the forms of art becomes relatively unimportant. In all the great formative periods of architecture a single style was exemplified in every type of building. Thus, in the Renaissance period in Italy, the same Classic convention expresses itself in divers ways. In a church, for instance, the walls might show an exterior surface of stone, brick, or stucco, but this made little or no difference to the composition of the façade either in respect of the window openings or of its decorative treatment, while inside the church, screens, pulpits, baldachinos, often made of stone, wood, plaster, or bronze, were not allowed to depart from the Classic style. Similarly the architecture of mediæval times, which is sometimes exalted as a praiseworthy example of the truthful expression of construction, follows exactly the same rule, and in the great Gothic cathedrals an exact correspondence prevails between the style of the stone exterior and that of the woodwork in the interior. The mediæval designers had not the smallest scruple in reproducing in their wooden screens arched forms similar to those which appeared in the stone walls, notwithstanding the fact that in wood a pointed arch, or indeed any other arch, has not the smallest structural justification. It is important to establish the similarity of the Classic and Gothic styles in respect of independence of materials, because it is a point which is generally missed. In fact, the theory so often propagated, that style is born of the adaptation to materials, might almost be reversed in favour of a declaration that the first and most characteristic mark of a true architectural style is that a manner of building has arisen in the determination of which the choice of materials plays a quite subordinate part.

While the main achievement of the Classic Order is the creation of an organic union between post and beam, it has also acquired renown as the parent of a system of mouldings and architectural ornament. In saying that the Classic Order vindicates the necessity of ornament and mouldings, one is not ascribing to these elements a merely decorative function, for the examples which will be discussed in the subsequent pages will prove that ornament enters into the very essence of the composition, and when once this fact is grasped a style of building divorced from mouldings and ornament can never again be contemplated with satisfaction. Any such style, however it may be described and whatever airs it may give itself, will surely be condemned as sectarian. For those who have eaten of the tree of knowledge and have acquired from the Greeks an understanding of ornament can never relinquish this very powerful aid to architectural composition.

Just as an architectural style is in a large measure independent of materials, it is also independent of climate. Since most of the weight of the attack upon the Classic Order from the mediævalist side is directed to the establishment of the proposition that the classic style is not suitable for a northern climate, it is perhaps worth while to point out that there is no architectural feature designed to protect buildings from cold or rain which is outside the repertory of the Classic style. Moreover, it must be borne in mind that in nearly the whole of what is known as the temperate zone, which happens to be that part of the earth's surface where the world's great architecture has been created, the temperature varies often as much as fifty degrees between summer and winter. A building would be given a quite impossible task were it expected in its style to be one thing in the height of summer and quite a different thing in the depth of winter. Again, one must inquire what are the characteristics of buildings designed for different climatic conditions. The windows seem to be the principal elements which need to be considered in this connection. Windows may be large or small, and they may or may not be provided with overhangs in the shape of hoods or canopies. It is obvious, however, that the style of architecture cannot be influenced by the size of the windows, because even in the same building one window is often much larger than another, and not even the most fanatical of those who advocate the dependence of style upon function or climate would contend that in the same building different window forms should be designed in different styles. Here, again, an analogy from mediæval architecture is useful, for it is notorious that the narrow lancet windows of the early English period have a stylistic affinity with the very large windows in the "lantern" churches of the fifteenth century, for both are rightly described as Gothic.

Fig. 1.—THE PROPYLÆA, ATHENS.

Showing the External Doric Order and the Internal Ionic Order.

There is one last quality of the Order which may be touched upon here—namely, its capacity to aid the establishment of a hierarchy of social values in the realm of architecture. And in discussing this question a comparison between architecture and dress may serve to point the argument. Dress, as everybody knows, is a reflection of manners, and by its convention supports a complicated order of society.

Dress provides the means of marking out certain types of persons for distinction, so that the participants in various social functions are recognised and set apart from others not so engaged, and this convention serves the public convenience. It is to the general advantage, for instance, that in a Law Court the judge should be marked by special habiliments so that he may be recognised by all present, while at a municipal function it is well that the mayor should be distinguished by his mayoral robes, and so on. It is a common complaint against the Classic Order that it is so often applied to a building as if it were a garment, but this statement need not imply disparagement of the Order if the garment be chosen with judgment and worn with distinction. That certain buildings are for social reasons given the privilege of having columns, increases the significance of such buildings as have not. The Order is not only a system of architectural composition which solves innumerable problems, but in addition to this it has a ceremonial quality with which civic architecture can ill dispense.

FIG. 2.—THE MAISON CARRÉE, NÎMES.
DETAIL OF THE EXTERNAL CORINTHIAN ORDER.
(*See also Plate XIX.*)

CHAPTER II

THE GREEK ORDERS

Before attempting an analysis of the æsthetic quality of the Order it may be as well to preface such a discussion by a very brief historical note. In the present context there is no object in entering at length into an examination of the archæological data which have been so exhaustively dealt with in authoritative treatises. Suffice it to say that long previous to the advent of the great civilisation of Greece the Egyptians had established a system of Orders, and recent investigations at the stepped pyramid at Sakkara have exposed a more developed type of proto-Doric Order than the well-known and often cited example at Beni-Hassan. At Knossos in Crete examples of post and beam have also been found which possess some of the qualities of the Order.

It was not until the seventh century B.C. that the Doric column became standardised in a form which in essentials was retained for hundreds of years, and eventually reached a degree of perfection exemplified in the Parthenon at Athens erected in the fifth century B.C. The Ionic Order should be regarded as a development which proceeded on parallel lines to the Doric, and its beginnings have been traced to Asia Minor. It has been conjectured that the distinctive form of the capital was originally derived from the painting of scrolls upon a primitive cushion capital. During the age of Pericles, when the buildings on the Acropolis at Athens were rebuilt, the Ionic Order was transplanted to the mainland and was set side by side with the Doric. The origin of the Corinthian Order cannot be determined so accurately as that of the other two types. The first examples of it which are known to archæological research show a high standard of development, for there is no record of the transitional stages through which it must have previously passed. The most famous Greek example is that of the small choragic monument of Lysicrates set up at Athens in 335 B.C. (Plate XI.). It is supposed that the Corinthian Order is derived from the pre-classical civilisations of Egypt and Assyria where many bell capitals of the same family as the Corinthian have been discovered. The Greeks evidently regarded the Corinthian column as an elaborate form of architectural support to be reserved for building of a highly ornate character, and it is certain that they never used it extensively.

In the developed or perfected Doric Order the column is of a singularly graceful and expressive shape. The square abacus of the capital acts as a transition between the round section of the column and the rectangular soffit of the architrave above it. The profile of the echinus unites the summit of the column to the abacus, and these elements not only provide a punctuation to the upper terminal of the column but contribute to its inflection. The Doric column differs from the Ionic and the Corinthian in being without a separate articulated base to the column itself. This apparent lack of punctuation at the base of the Doric column has occasionally been instanced in support of an argument that the principle of punctuation has here been successfully defied. It must be borne in mind, however, that the Doric column, as seen in Greek examples, invariably stands on a stylobate, and while this latter is not inflected to take account of each individual column, it serves as a collective base for the colonnade as a whole. Moreover, and this is a very important point, the entasis of the Doric column helps to inflect its form, for by its means the base of the column, being of considerably larger girth than the summit, is adequately differentiated from it, and the contour of the entasis itself constitutes yet another inflection.

The curve of the entasis is so very slight that it is impossible to dogmatise concerning the mathematical construction which was actually employed by the Greeks. It has been alleged by Penrose and other investigators that the curve employed was a conic section, either a parabola or a hyperbola. Such a statement, however, which is probably due to the fact that conic sections were the only mathematical curves known to the investigators themselves, is not based upon any consideration of the æsthetic quality of the curves in question. After all, there is no special merit in a section of a parabola or hyperbola in architectural composition unless the curve is in some way related to its environment. If the kind of curve which would have such an æsthetic relationship to the base and summit of the column is considered, the curve would need, of course, to be at a critical point of its progression both at the base and at the summit. Assume that at the base the profile starts in a true vertical direction and immediately begins to bend inwards very slightly and at a certain rate. Let this rate of bending decrease at a uniform rate so that at the top of the column the curve has become straight and is, in fact, about to bend the other way. In such an instance a curve results which is sensitive to its environment, for at its base its direction is at right angles to the platform upon which it rests while at the summit it is at the critical point of its career when its curvature is zero. To a person who has trained his eye to appreciate the æsthetic quality of curves, a curve so constructed would give satisfaction, and it appears that the entasis used by the Greeks was neither a parabola nor hyperbola, but a curve of the character above described.

In the case of the Doric column, in which there is a greater difference of girth between base and summit than in the Ionic or Corinthian, the entasis plays a more important part, and in fact gives the shape of the column a degree of vitality which enables it to dispense with the separate articulated base invariably used with the other Orders. While the entasis has the definite æsthetic purpose of inflecting the contour of a column, and is intended to be visible and obvious, other curves which the Greeks introduced in the lines of their temple buildings were designed to correct certain optical illusions. For instance, the steps of the stylobate were given a very slight curvature, convex towards the ground, and this served to counteract a certain effect of sagging which might otherwise have been apparent. Another refinement exemplified in the Parthenon was the very slight tilting of the axes of the columns towards a common centre, and although this is scarcely noticeable, even to a careful observer, it adds an element of distinction to the composition and provides yet one more evidence of the subtlety of mind which the Greeks brought to bear upon their architecture.

The Doric entablature has also a certain subtlety which is absent from that of the Ionic and Corinthian, due to the alternation of triglyphs and metopes. Whether or not the triglyphs owe their origin to the form of wooden ceiling rafters which rested upon a wooden beam or architrave, there is no question that they give an additional beauty to the frieze which by their means inflects itself to take notice of the columns beneath it. And as has often been pointed out, the relative disposition of triglyphs and metopes enables the frieze to adjust itself to the occasion when the inter-columniation of the end columns in a temple is less than that of the intermediate columns. By placing the angle triglyph at the end of the frieze instead of having its axis central with that of the column, the interval between the corner triglyph and that two spaces away is appropriately reduced. This lessening of the inter-columniation at the angles, which has wrongly been given a constructional justification, is in reality but another example of the principle of punctuation ; for the row of columns which in its central portion proceeds by regular intervals, when it is about to come to a conclusion shows itself to be aware of this fact by breaking the sequence. The principle of punctuation might have been just as well exemplified if the end interval had been made a little wider than the others, but while in the case of the temple there are constructional reasons which justify the smaller interval, one can easily imagine a type of building in which a wider interval at the ends of a row of columns or posts might appear elegant.

The entablature comprises the architrave or bearing member immediately above the columns, the frieze or central member, and the cornice. A very important development of this latter feature is the *pediment*, in which two sloping cornices in alignment with the verges of the roof are cleverly united by a horizontal member comprising only the lower portion of the cornice. The triangular space within the pediment provides an ideal position for sculpture. The cornice is an æsthetic element which is needed as a punctuation of the upper terminal of the wall. For the wall must not appear as if it had come to a conclusion suddenly. Just as the capital is the head of the column, so the cornice is the head of the wall considered as a whole.

The parallel of the Greek and Roman Orders given on Plate II. shows clearly that the prototypes invented by the Greeks were not departed from in any essential by the Romans, who were held, as it were, in an intellectual enthralment by the Order. Certain qualities of the Greek Doric Order have already been discussed, and, as far as the main characteristics of the association of column and entablature are concerned, there is no essential difference between it and the Ionic and Corinthian types. In the latter, the columns are more slender, and in proportion the entablature is of less vertical dimension than in the Doric. Between the Ionic and Corinthian entablatures there appears no essential difference, and it is by the capitals that these Orders are most easily recognised. And it is a tribute to the perfection of form of these terminal ornaments that of the thousands of designers who have practised the classic style during the last two thousand years so few have considered themselves capable of devising a type of capital superior to either of these. The most perfect Greek Ionic capital from the Erechtheum is given on Plate VII., and the Order as a whole is of exquisite refinement. It will be observed that the frieze is sculptured, but in spite of this the serenity of the composition is preserved intact. It is one of the unique qualities of the Classic Order that its decorative elements can achieve extraordinary richness and elaboration without sacrificing the simplicity and vigour of the composition as a whole. Two other examples of the Greek Ionic Order are illustrated on Plates VI. and VIII., and the anta capital at Cnidus is of peculiar interest, inasmuch as it shows a special pilaster type which provided a significant variation from the column capital. Plate IX., which shows the Temple of Apollo at Bassæ, is a unique example, because the capital is especially designed for the interior of the building where it can only be seen from a very short distance away, while the spreading base seems adapted to a position where there is no stylobate. Plates X., XI., and XII. give three famous examples of

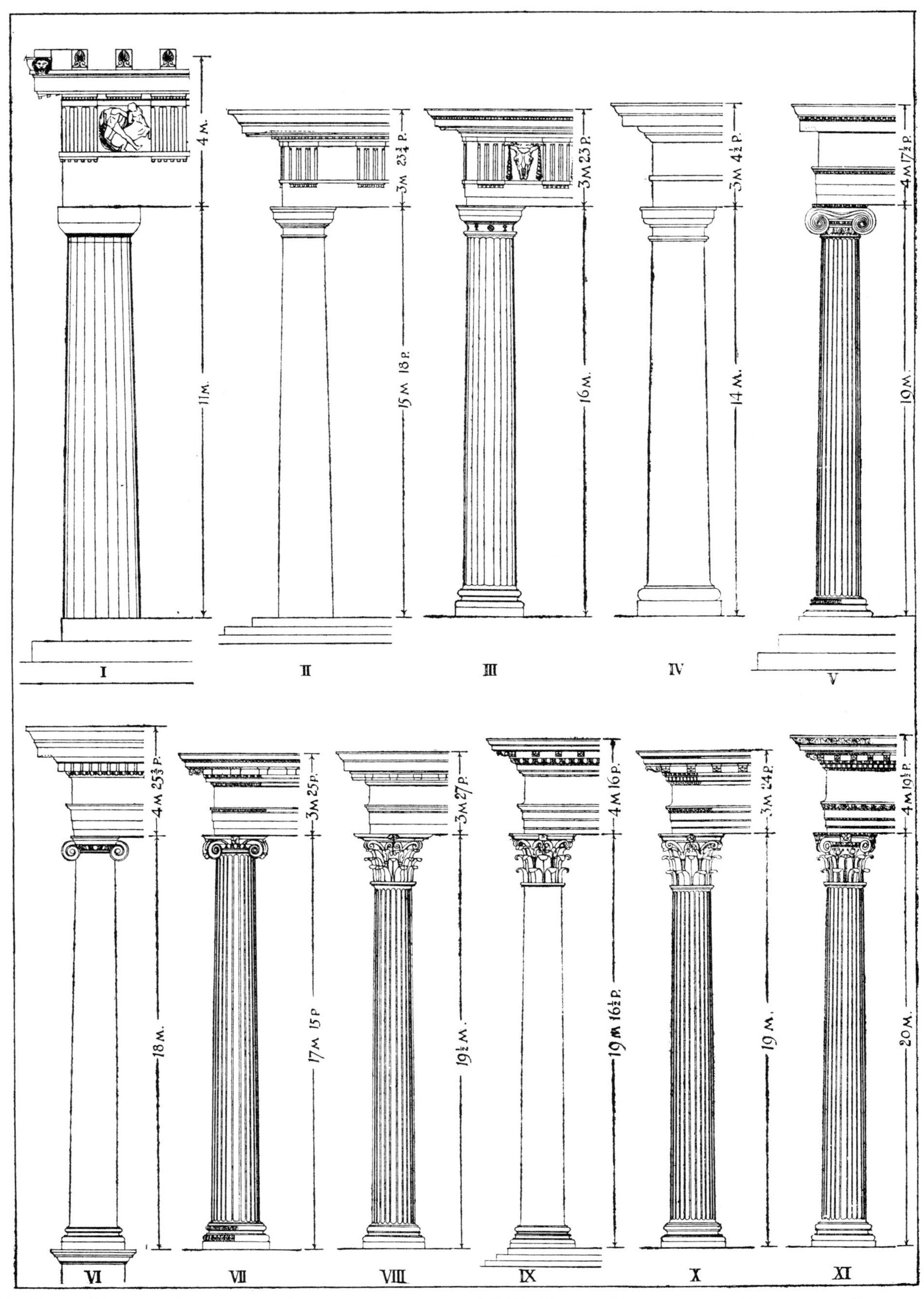

I. Greek Doric. Parthenon, Athens.
II. Roman Doric. Theatre of Marcellus, Rome.
III. Italian Doric. After Palladio.
IV. Italian Tuscan. After Palladio.
V. Greek Ionic. Erechtheum, Athens.
VI. Roman Ionic. Theatre of Marcellus, Rome.
VII. Italian Ionic. After Scamozzi.
VIII. Greek Corinthian. Temple of Jupiter Olympius, Athens.
IX. Roman Corinthian. Pantheon, Rome.
X. Italian Corinthian. After Palladio.
XI. Roman Composite. The Thermæ of Diocletian, Rome.

the Greek Corinthian Order, all of which have been re-used innumerable times. In the Corinthian capital the ornamentation does not seem to weaken the structural competence of the capital, because it so obviously lies upon the surface of the bell, and herein lies the reason of its complete success. Plate XIII. shows to a larger scale some exquisite examples of Greek ornament, now so familiar that it is difficult to realise what must have been the artistic delight of those who first originated them.

FIG. 3.—CAPITAL FROM ELEUSIS.

CHAPTER III

THE ROMAN ORDERS

It is customary when comparing Greek and Roman architecture to do less than justice to the architectural genius of the Romans. Yet but for them the Classic Order might have died a premature death. It is to the credit of the Romans that their artistic judgment enabled them to appreciate the Order and understand that it could be the basis of a style extraordinarily useful to themselves. Their main contribution to architecture was that they took the Classic Order and associated it with the arch, and in so doing they gave to both of these features an enhanced vitality.

The semicircular arch is, of course, a perfect geometric form which has the elegance that is derived from a complete organic unity. This unity, however, is, as it were, self-contained, and it does not follow that it can necessarily take its place harmoniously as a subordinate part of an architectural composition. The arch is round, but the façades in which it is placed have generally a rectangular outline. Consequently it would seem to require some kind of a rectangular frame if it is to have an æsthetic relationship to the façade of a building. It is the quality of the Classic Order that it provides a rectangular framework of a highly distinguished and ceremonial kind.

One might almost imagine that the arch and the Order were from the first destined for matrimony. Yet strange as it may seem, the Romans have been criticised for encouraging this union, for it is urged against them that by associating it with the arch they made of the Classic Order an element of decoration and divorced it from what was supposed to be its structural purpose. Yet the theorists who advance such an objection in the same breath are apt to speak slightingly of the Romans as a race of engineers. These engineers, nevertheless, had the intellectual perception which enabled them to realise that the function of the Order is primarily an æsthetic one.

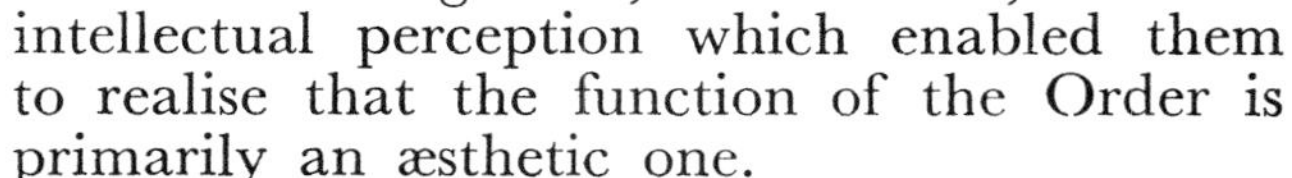

Fig. 4.—ARCH OF TITUS, ROME.

In the great commemorative arches which must be counted among the principal architectural achievements of the Romans it is obvious that the applied Order is doing no structural work whatsoever (Plate xxiii. and Fig. 4). But it succeeds in giving to the arch a remarkable degree of vitality. It will be observed that the mouldings of the architrave, which are to be found in the horizontal beams above the columns of a Greek temple, are skilfully bent round to form a distinguished punctuation to the arch itself, increasing the degree of its self-consciousness. By this architrave the wall surface is *inflected*, so that before the aperture really begins the wall seems to be prepared for it. At the summit of the arch, where alone the curve is in a horizontal direction and parallel to the architrave of the Order above, a decorative keystone occurs which helps to give the arch æsthetic stability, and unites it to the rectangular framework in which it is enclosed. Another critical point in the curve of the arch occurs at its base, where for one brief moment its lines are in a vertical direction and concur with the lines of the jambs of the arch. At these points, therefore, it is fitting that there should be some formal recognition by the wall surface itself, and this is achieved by a subsidiary cornice at the imposts of the arch. This short length of cornice performs no structural work, yet it not only stops the curved architrave, but in another way it increases the vitality of the composition, for by its means the curve of the arch does not slide unceremoniously into the jambs beneath, but achieves this transition with an artistic flourish most pleasant to behold. Again, it will be observed that in both of the triumphal arches illustrated on Plate XXIII.—namely, those of Septimius Severus and of Constantine—the line of the impost of the major arch is taken up on either side by a string course, which performs an exactly similar function for the subsidiary arches on either side as does the architrave of the Order for the central opening. Again, these small arches are given architraves appropriate to their size, and these are stopped with small cornices or cappings at the level of the imposts, while the heads of the arches are united to the strings above them by decorative keystones. The grandeur of this composition must surely impress anyone capable of reading the language of architecture. Yet if these arches are stripped of the whole paraphernalia of the Order—and one imagines what they would look like if they were formed of solid stone of the same size and shape as in these examples, and pierced by arches of the same dimension—the subtlety and distinction of the design would be entirely sacrificed.

Fig. 5.—ROMAN ENTABLATURE.
From a Sixteenth-Century Original Drawing.

Critics of the Classic Order—who now contend that this feature is out of date, on the ground that twentieth-century methods of construction have made it supererogatory—had they lived in the time of the ancient Romans, would equally have scoffed at the grand ceremonial arches, or the external façade of the Coliseum and the Theatre of Marcellus, for in these examples the Order is applied and does no structural work. They would have proved themselves to be obstructionists, who, if they had had their way, would have strangled the noble architecture of the Romans at its birth. It is a misnomer to describe the applied Order of the arch of Septimius, for instance, as merely decorative, for it is far more than that. Decorative indeed it is, but the Order is here the means of giving to the composition an organic unity by virtue of which it becomes architecture.

Two important distinctions may be observed in a comparison between the Greek and Roman use of the Order. In a point where the Greek style was flexible, the Roman became rigid, and in another point, where the Greek style appeared a little timid and conservative, the Roman showed an amazing resource and fertility of invention. In their treatment of the Order itself the Greeks for ever remained experimentalists, and no two examples created by them are quite the same; yet they created few variations in the major compositions in which the Order is set out. In fact, one cannot visit the Acropolis to-day without feeling that a single type of building with pediment is repeated *ad nauseam*, and that the juxtaposition of big temples and small temples of similar shape does not represent a very high standard of civic design. The Romans, however, were city builders on a large scale, and their enormous power and wealth enabled them to erect structures fulfilling a far greater variety of social functions than were to be found among the Greeks. Consequently their inventive talents were directed to another channel, and in the planning and composition of large buildings they found scope for an artistic talent truly remarkable. They would not have been free, however, to develop their architecture in this direction had they at the same time been making too many experiments with the Order. They were content to accept the Order as an accomplished fact. They stabilised it, standardised it, yet never lost sight of its true æsthetic function.

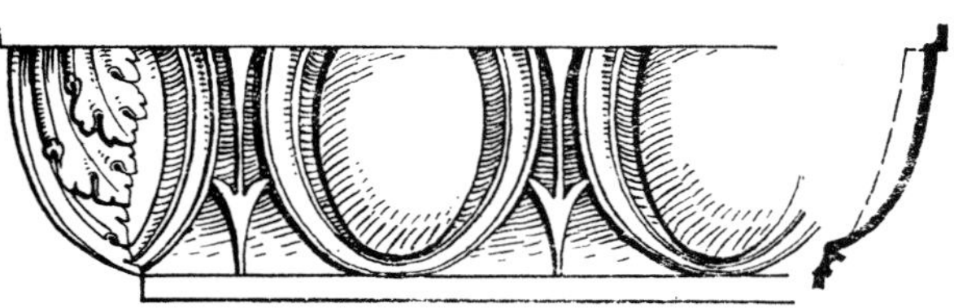

Fig. 6.—ROMAN EGG AND DART ENRICHMENT.

The Roman Orders, nevertheless, differ markedly in some minor respects from the Greek, and perhaps one may even venture to affirm that they represent certain improvements. This may perhaps seem a sacrilegious statement, for it has so often been affirmed that the Order of the Parthenon, for instance, is without blemish. If it is compared, however, with the Roman Doric Order of the Theatre of Marcellus (Plates II. and XV.), it is observable that in comparison with the frieze the architrave has been reduced in dimension. May it not be argued that the Roman example has a certain additional merit in that it avoids the equality between the architrave and the frieze apparent in the Parthenon? It is true, of course, that with the addition of the cornice the entablature becomes a trinitarian composition. Nevertheless, the two lower members are so clearly differentiated from the cornice that one can scarcely help reading them together as a sub-unit in themselves. Consequently a measure of discord arises if these members are of equal vertical dimension and compete with one another. In the Roman example the frieze is noticeably taller than the architrave, and, moreover, the cornice itself has a more gradual over-sail, and is thus brought more closely into relationship with what lies underneath it. The Doric Order, according to Vignola (Plates XXIX.-XXXIII.), carries the process still further, and this is of great interest, inasmuch as it shows that the great Italian architect—who was undoubtedly acquainted with the Parthenon—shared the view of the ancient Romans that the Doric entablature required to be improved in this respect.

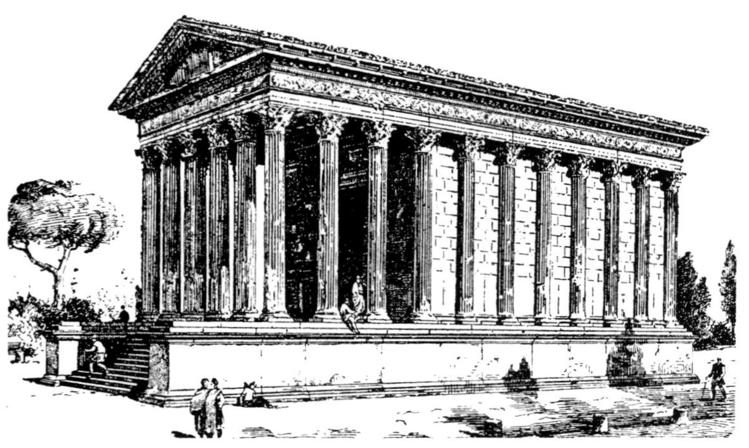

Fig. 7.—THE MAISON CARRÉE, NÎMES.

For not only did the frieze deepen still further, but the architrave is broken up so that its subordination to the frieze is made more emphatic. Akin to the Roman Doric is the Tuscan Order which, according to Vitruvius, was derived from Greek sources—that is to say, its originators, although settled in Italy, were of Greek descent. This was an Order of simple parts (Plates XXV.-XXVIII.), in which, however, the column has an element of elaboration lacking in the Greek Doric inasmuch as it is provided with an articulated base.

The Romans also introduced certain variations into the Ionic and Corinthian Orders. In these the differences are not so marked, although it is observable that the cornice of the Roman Ionic Order at the theatre of Marcellus (Plate XVI.) is in proportion much greater than it is in either the Erechtheum (Plate VII.) or the temple of Athena Polias at Priene (Plate VIII.). Perhaps this is due to the fact that the Romans were gradually detaching the cornice from the entablature and using it independently for a large number of architectural occasions, and were realising its effectiveness as a punctuating member in the upper terminals of large buildings. The Romans made a very important contribution to the development of the cornice and imparted to this feature a grandeur and impressiveness not to be found in Greek exemplars (Fig. 5). The Corinthian Order, which was used but little by the Greeks, appealed strongly to the Romans, who delighted in its highly decorative qualities. Here, again, the cornice grew in dimension and in the richness and elaboration of its parts. In the temple of Castor and Pollux, for instance (Plates XX. and XXI.), the cornice is as deep as frieze and architrave put together, and there is no question that the result is highly satisfactory.

The ambition of the Romans to prove their originality in the treatment of the Orders led them to devise a new Order called the Composite, whereby they hoped to add to their architectural fame. It is noteworthy, however, that in this task of exploration they proceeded with extreme caution, for they did not venture to create an Order which differed as much from the standard ones—namely, the Doric, Ionic, and Corinthian—as these did from each other, but were content to design what may be described as a hybrid Order which was, in point of fact, a not very satisfactory mixture of the Ionic and Corinthian. It is principally in the capital of the column that the Composite Order is distinguished from its predecessors, for the foliated bell of the Corinthian cap is surmounted by Ionic volutes. The Composite Order is richly decorated and cannot be said to be altogether a failure because in its main proportions it does not depart from the tried and established conventions of the older Orders. But, on the other hand, it is not an important innovation, and has always been treated by architects themselves as occupying a very small place in their repertory. It is of interest to note, however, that Palladio, on occasion, used the Composite Order (Plate LIV.), and Sir Christopher Wren employed it in the upper stage of the façades of St Paul's Cathedral.

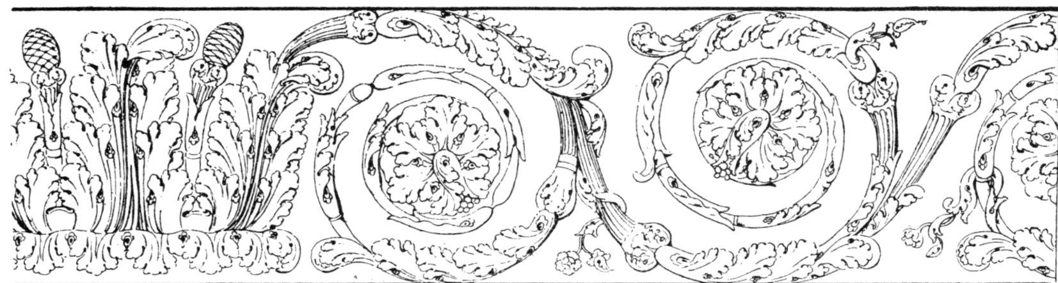

FIG. 8.—DETAIL OF THE CARVED FRIEZE OF THE EXTERNAL CORINTHIAN ORDER, MAISON CARRÉE, NÎMES.

Annotated List of Plates

SECTION I

THE ORDERS OF CLASSICAL ANTIQUITY

THE GREEK ORDERS

Plate I.—Frontispiece.

THE DORIC ORDER OF THE PARTHENON, ATHENS, from a water-colour sketch, *c.* 1818, in the possession of the Author, by Lewis Vulliamy.

A PARALLEL OF THE ORDERS

Plate II.

I. GREEK DORIC. Parthenon, Athens. (See also Plates I., III., IV.)
II. ROMAN DORIC. Theatre of Marcellus, Rome. (See also Plates XIV., XV., XVI.)
III. ITALIAN DORIC. After Palladio.
IV. ITALIAN TUSCAN. After Palladio.
V. GREEK IONIC. Erechtheum, Athens. (See also Plates VI., XIII.)
VI. ROMAN IONIC. Theatre of Marcellus, Rome. (See also Plates XIV., XV., XVI.)
VII. ITALIAN IONIC. After Scamozzi.
VIII. GREEK CORINTHIAN. Temple of Jupiter Olympius, Athens.
IX. ROMAN CORINTHIAN. Pantheon, Rome. (See also Plate XVIII.)
X. ITALIAN CORINTHIAN. After Palladio.
XI. ROMAN COMPOSITE. Thermæ of Diocletian, Rome. (See also Plate XXII.)

GREEK DORIC ORDER

Plate III.—THE PARTHENON, ATHENS, 454-438 B.C. The most perfect of all Grecian temples, built of Pentelic marble, by Ictinus and Callicrates, in the time of Pericles. Peripteral octastyle on plan, with seventeen columns on flanks and standing on a stylobate of three steps. Fluted columns of peristyle, 34 ft. 3 ins. high, dia. 6 ft. 2 ins., the angle columns having a dia. of 6 ft. 3½ ins. The Plate shows end of side elevation, section through entablature, part plan looking up, and method of drawing flutes.

Plate IV.—THE PARTHENON, ATHENS. Details of the Order. Entablature and capital, with section, and part plan looking up; perspective of angle; enlarged section through cornice and pediment, and profile of capital, with annulets.

Plate V.—DETAILS OF A DORIC COLONNADE AT CNIDUS, IONIA, with peristyle of an agora. The colonnade is possibly part of a stoa built by Sostrates, third century B.C. Both as restored from data obtained in discoveries, 1812. *Above*, part elevation of the agora peristyle. *Left*, Order of the agora peristyle. *Below*, hexastyle portico at end of colonnade.

GREEK IONIC ORDER

Plate VI.—IONIC PORTICO AT CNIDUS, IONIA, probably of the third century B.C. As restored from data obtained in discoveries, 1812. Two unfluted columns, 1 ft. 10 ins. dia., between antæ, which are of the same dimensions on two faces. *Centre*, elevation of portico. *Above*, capital of the Order. *Left*, detail of entablature, anta capital, and base. *Right*, section through the Order.

Plate VII.—ERECHTHEUM, ATHENS, *c.* 420 B.C. Mnesicles, architect. Built on two levels, it has three porticoes of different design and seems to have been a combination of two or three temples in one. This Plate gives the Order of the prostyle tetrastyle portico on the N. side. The capitals of the angle columns have angle volutes. Columns, 25 ft. high; dia. 2 ft. 9 ins.

Plate VIII.—TEMPLE OF ATHENA POLIAS, PRIENE, IONIA, 320 B.C. Peripteral hexastyle on plan, with eleven columns on flank. One of the few instances of the Greek Ionic Order with moulded base carried on a square die. Columns, 40 ft. 4½ ins. high; dia. 4 ft. 3 ins.

Plate IX.—Temple of Apollo Epicurius, Bassæ, 430 b.c. Ictinus, architect. Peripteral hexastyle. In this temple all three Greek Orders—Doric, Ionic, and Corinthian—are introduced. This Plate gives details of the distinctive Order of Ionic half-columns in the interior, five of which on each side are attached to short walls projecting into the naos. Columns, 25 ft. high; dia. 2 ft. $2\frac{3}{4}$ ins.

GREEK CORINTHIAN ORDER

Plate X.—The Tholos, Epidaurus, 350 b.c. A circular building with an external peristyle of twenty-six Doric columns, and a cella with a circle of fourteen Corinthian columns, standing free from the wall. This Plate gives details of the internal Order, with its beautiful capital and cornice designed for internal effect.

Plate XI.—The Choragic Monument of Lysicrates, Athens, 335 b.c. Small circular structure upon a square base 14 ft. high. The six Corinthian columns—complete and independent of the panels between them—rest on a circular moulded plinth. Columns, 11 ft. 7 ins. high; dia. 1 ft. 2 ins.

Plate XII.—The "Tower of the Winds," Athens, 100-35 b.c. Octagonal building on a stylobate of three steps. This Plate gives the Order of the porticoes on the N.E. and N.W. sides. The fluted columns have no bases and the capitals are of unusual type. Although possibly a debased Order, it has met with such general approval that it has been followed in many neo-classic buildings. Columns, 13 ft. 6 ins. high; dia. 1 ft. $7\frac{1}{2}$ ins.

GREEK ORNAMENT

Plate XIII.

I. Mausoleum, Halicarnassus. Upper member of cornice.
II. The Erechtheum, Athens. Detail of frieze.
III. The Tholos, Epidaurus. Detail of frieze along top of cella wall on peristyle side.
IV. Athens. Fragment of frieze, from the Acropolis.
V. The Erechtheum, Athens. Enrichments on mouldings of anta base.
VI. Athens. Cornice enrichments.

THE ROMAN ORDERS

ROMAN SUPERIMPOSED ORDERS

Plate XIV.—The Theatre of Marcellus, Rome, 23-13 b.c. Stone-built theatre, on a level site, with semicircular auditorium. Two tiers of outer arcading with superimposed Doric and Ionic Orders. Semi-attached columns on piers to both upper and lower tiers.

ROMAN DORIC ORDER

Plate XV.—The Theatre of Marcellus, Rome.—This Plate shows the Doric Order of the lower tier of outer arcading. (See also Plates xiv. and xvi.)

ROMAN IONIC ORDER

Plate XVI.—The Theatre of Marcellus, Rome. Ionic Order of the upper tier of outer arcading. (See also Plates xiv., xv.)

POMPEIAN ORDERS

Plate XVII.

I. The "Soldiers' Quarters," Pompeii. Doric Order of the colonnade. The columns were stuccoed and painted in colour, the lower part red.
II. The "House of the Tragic Poet," Pompeii. Doric Order from inner peristyle. Capital painted in colour; lower part of column painted red.
III. The "Triangular Forum," Pompeii. Ionic Order of entrance portico, 55 ft. 6 ins. in length and consisting of six columns between three-quarter respond columns and antæ.
IV. and V. Cornice and Capital from the "Triangular Forum."
VI. Another Ionic Capital, Pompeii. Originally covered with stucco and painted.

ROMAN CORINTHIAN ORDER

Plate XVIII.—The Portico of the Pantheon, Rome.—The portico, which belonged originally to a temple built by Agrippa, was taken down and, at a later date, re-erected, with eight columns in front instead of ten, as the frontispiece of Hadrian's Rotunda. Bases, capitals, and entablature of white Pentelic marble, shafts of granite, unfluted and monolithic. Columns, 46 ft. 5 ins. high ; dia. 4 ft. 11½ ins.

Plate XIX.—The Maison Carrée, Nîmes, A.D. 14. The best preserved Roman temple existing (Fig. 7). Raised on a podium 12 ft. high, it is hexastyle pseudo-peripteral, with a portico three columns deep, and semi-attached columns round the cella walls. Columns, 30 ft. 6 ins. high ; dia. 2 ft. 9 ins.

Plate XX.—The Temple of Castor and Pollux, Rome.—Perspective drawing of the Order. The capital is very fine ; the interlacing of the tendrils and the foliage rising between the volutes and running along the cavetto of the abacus are found only in this example. (See Plate xxi.)

Plate XXI.—The Temple of Castor and Pollux, Rome, formerly known as the Temple of Jupiter Stator. Built by Tiberius, A.D. 6. It is perhaps the finest Corinthian Order known, though rather exuberant in its carved ornament. Columns and entablature of Pentelic marble. Columns, 48 ft. 5 ins. high ; dia. 4 ft. 10 ins. Three columns only remain standing.

ROMAN COMPOSITE ORDER

Plate XXII.

I. The Triumphal Arch of Septimius Severus, Rome, A.D. 204. Composite Order of four detached fluted columns on each front, standing on pedestals and with pilasters behind them. Columns, 27 ft. 10 ins. high ; dia. 2 ft. 10½ ins. (See Plate xxiii. for application of Order.)

II. Thermæ of Diocletian, Rome, A.D. 302. Order of the four central columns of the tepidarium : converted by Michelangelo in 1563 into the church of S.M. degli Angeli. Monolithic granite shafts with capitals of white marble. Columns, 50 ft. high ; dia. 5 ft.

ROMAN TRIUMPHAL ARCHES

Plate XXIII.—*Above*, Arch of Septimius Severus, Rome. Built to commemorate Parthian victories. Triple arch type, of Pentelic marble. (For detail of Order see Plate xxii.)

Below, The Arch of Constantine, Rome, A.D. 312. Built to commemorate victory over Maxentius. Many of the reliefs are from an earlier Arch of Trajan. Triple arch type. Four detached monolithic and fluted columns on each front stand on high pedestals. Columns, 27 ft. 4 ins. high ; dia. 2 ft. 11 ins.

ROMAN ORNAMENT

Plate XXIV.

I. and III. From The Temple of the Sun, Rome. Fragments now in the Colonna Gardens.
II. From The Forum of Trajan, Rome. Entablature.
IV. From The Temple of Vespasian, Rome. Architrave enrichment.
V. From The Temple of Concord, Rome. Architrave enrichment.
VI. From The Column of Trajan, Rome. Enrichment of capital and necking.
VII. From The Temple of Mars the Avenger, Rome. Dado frieze of portico.

Fig. 9.

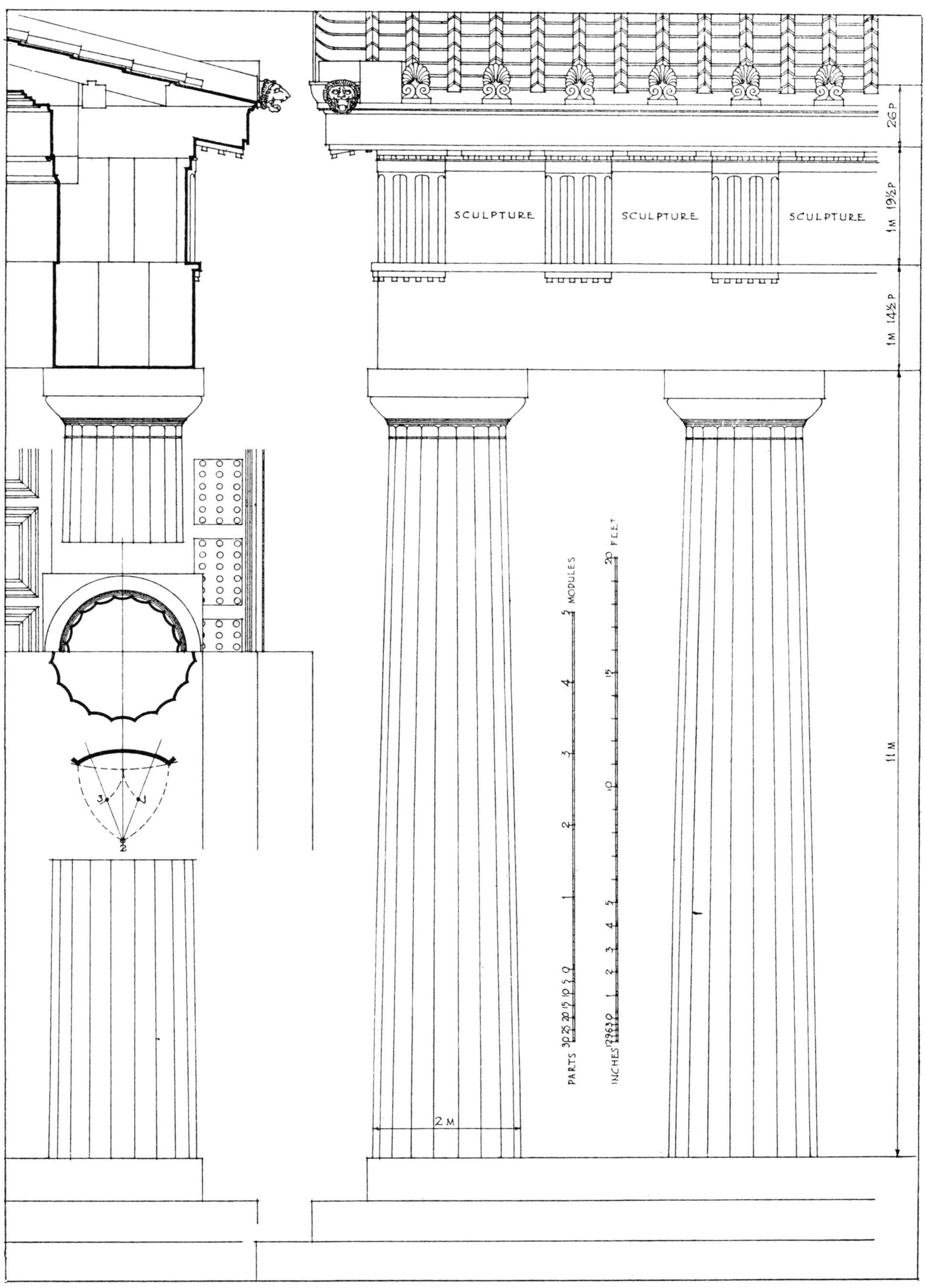

THE PARTHENON, ATHENS.

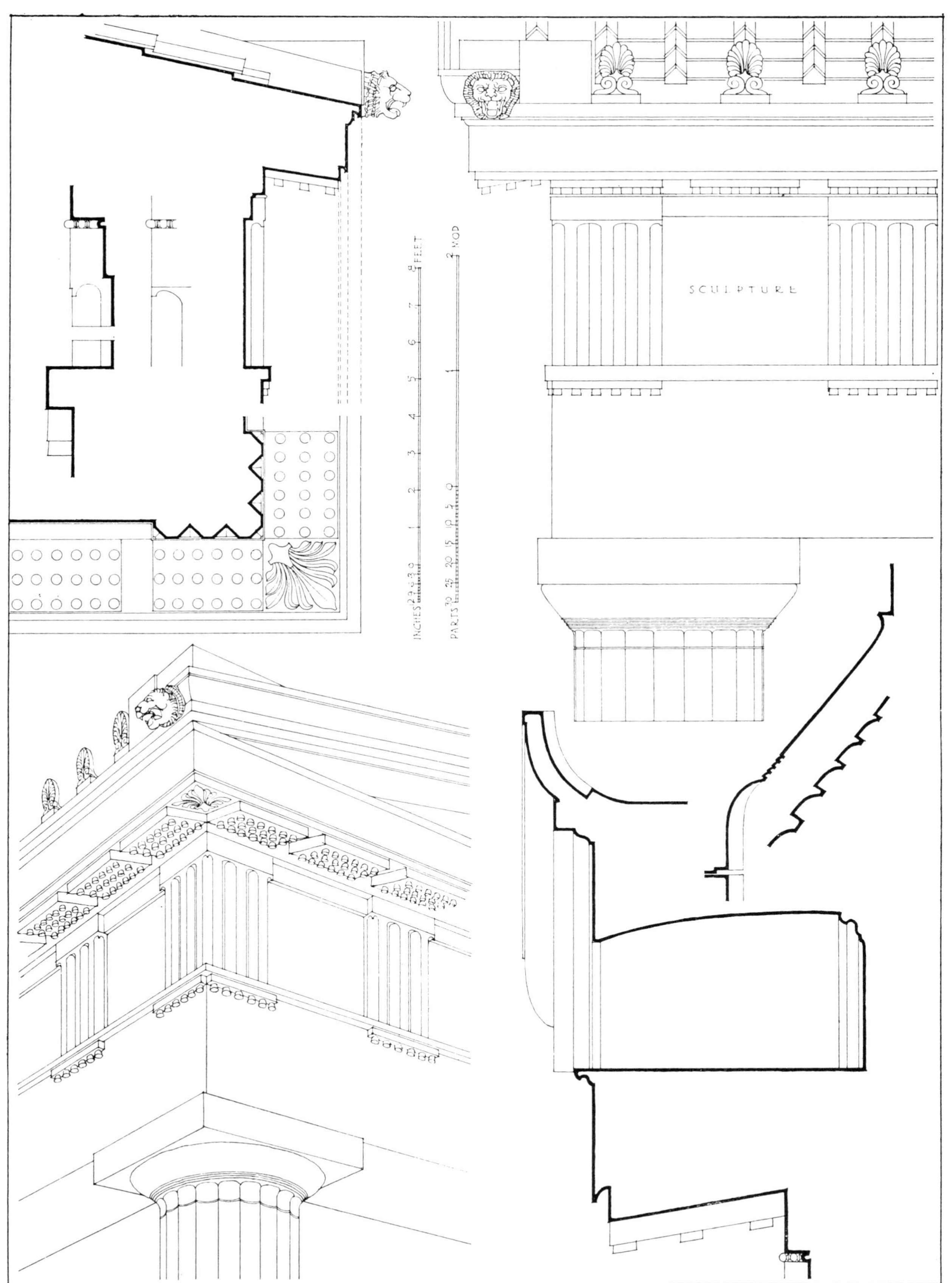

DETAILS OF THE PARTHENON, ATHENS.

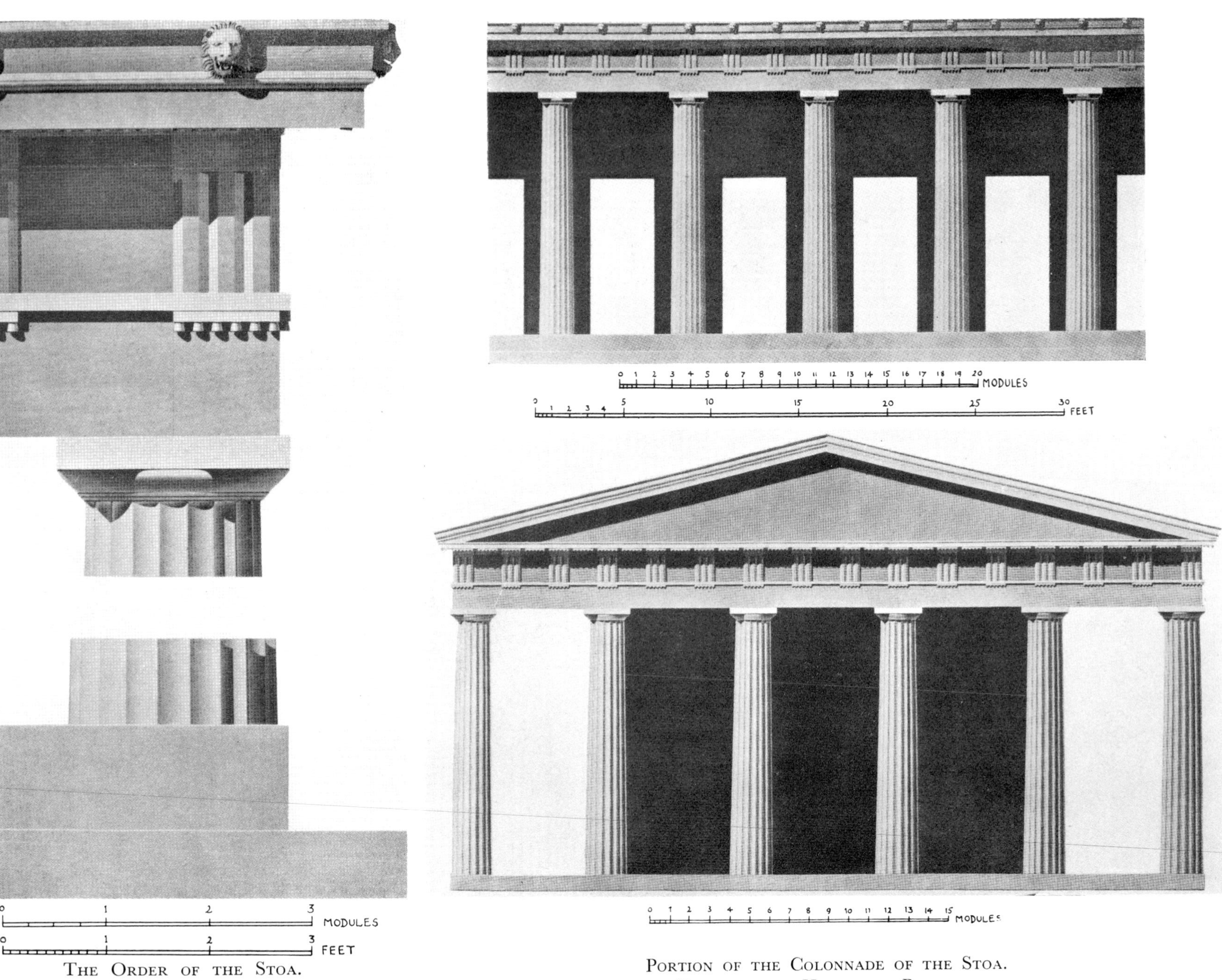

THE ORDER OF THE STOA.

PORTION OF THE COLONNADE OF THE STOA.
ELEVATION OF HEXASTYLE PORTICO.

CNIDUS, IONIA.

GREEK IONIC ORDER.

Detail of Anta and Entablature.

Ionic Portico and Detail of Capital.

Section through the Order.

CNIDUS, IONIA.

THE ERECHTHEUM, ATHENS.
THE ORDER OF THE TETRASTYLE PORTICO ON THE NORTH SIDE.

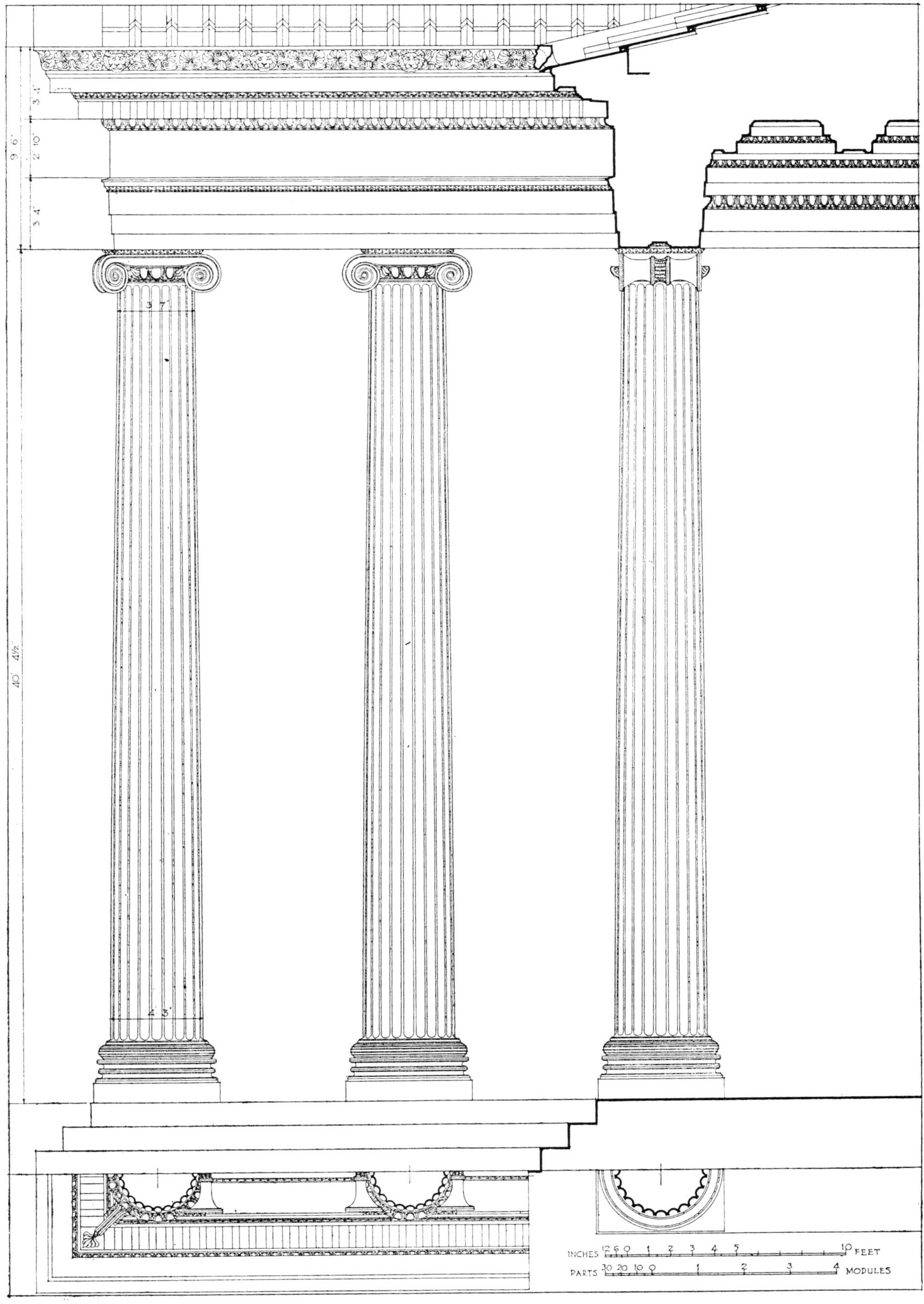

TEMPLE OF ATHENA POLIAS, PRIENE.

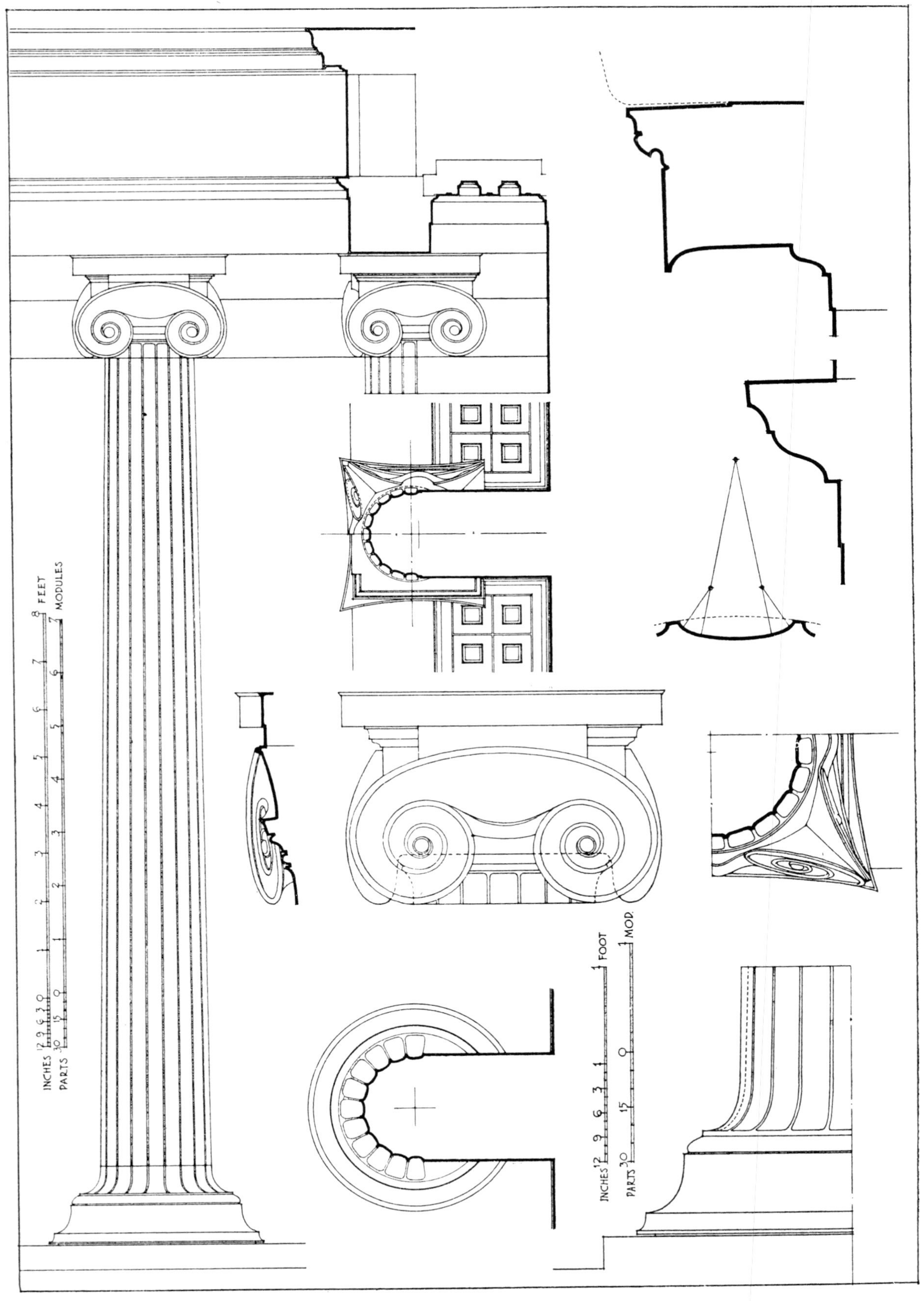

TEMPLE OF APOLLO EPICURIUS, BASSÆ.

GREEK CORINTHIAN ORDER.

THE INTERNAL ORDER OF THE THOLOS, EPIDAURUS.

THE CHORAGIC MONUMENT OF LYSICRATES, ATHENS.

THE "TOWER OF THE WINDS," ATHENS.

I.

III.

IV.

II.

V.

VI.

I. FROM THE MAUSOLEUM, HALICARNASSUS. UPPER MEMBER OF CORNICE.
II. FROM THE ERECHTHEUM, FRIEZE.
III. FROM EPIDAURUS, FRIEZE.
IV. FROM ATHENS, FRAGMENT OF FRIEZE.
V. FROM THE ERECHTHEUM, GUILLOCHE ON TORUS OF BASE.
VI. FROM ATHENS, FRAGMENT. *James Cromar Watt, del.*

I.-V. From Restorations edited by H. D'Espouy.

THE THEATRE OF MARCELLUS, ROME.

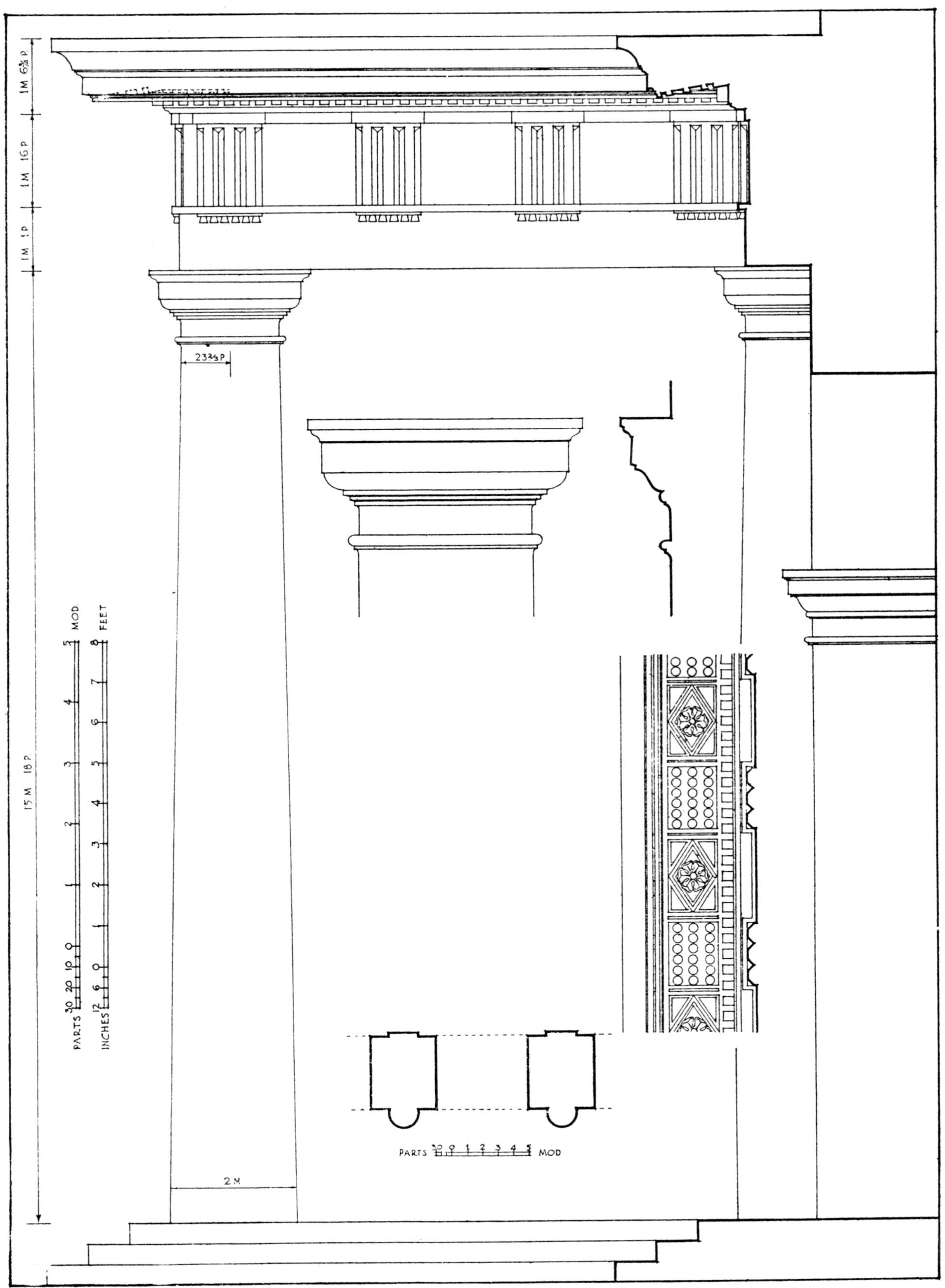

THE THEATRE OF MARCELLUS, ROME

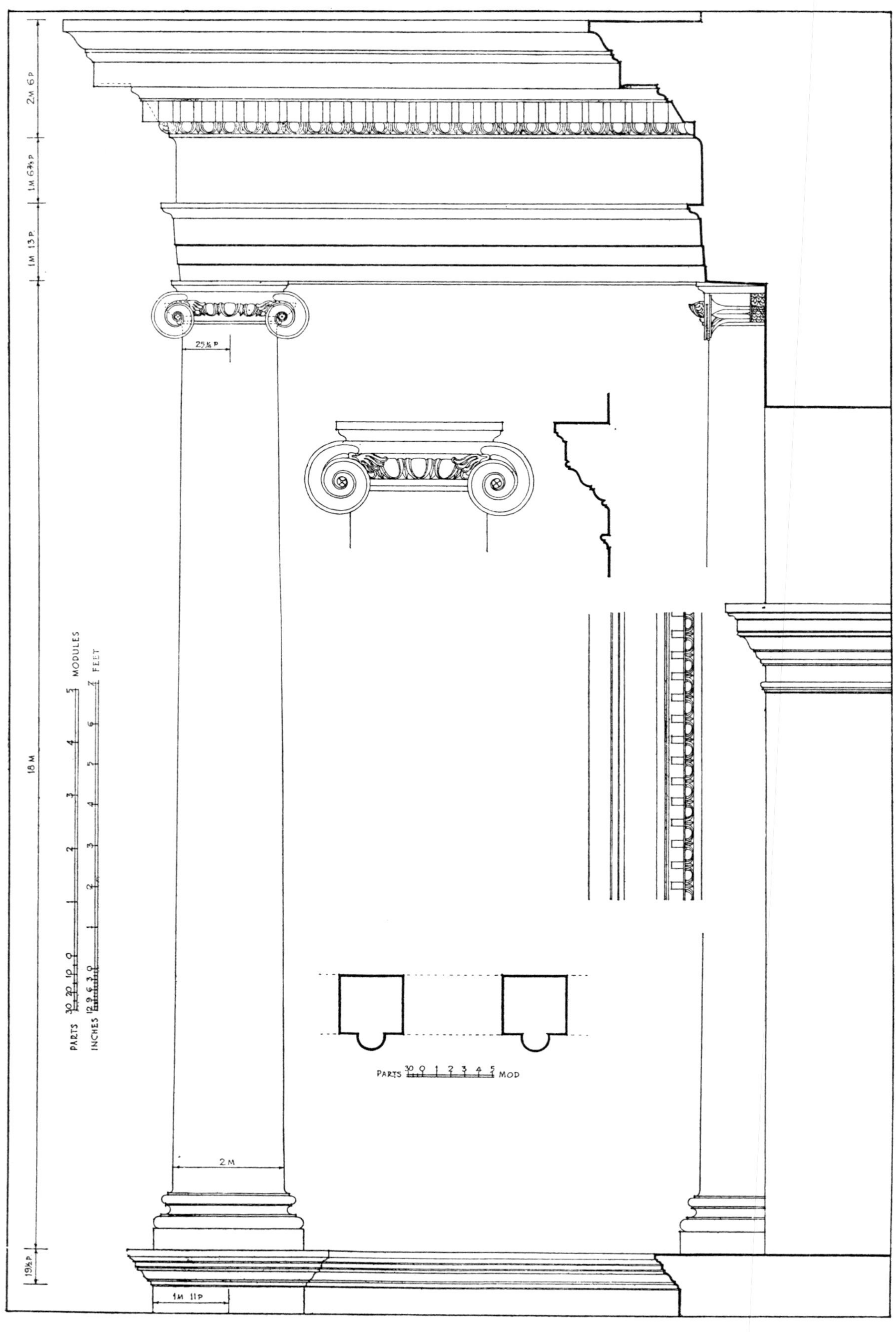

THE THEATRE OF MARCELLUS, ROME.

POMPEIAN ORDERS.

Plate XVII.

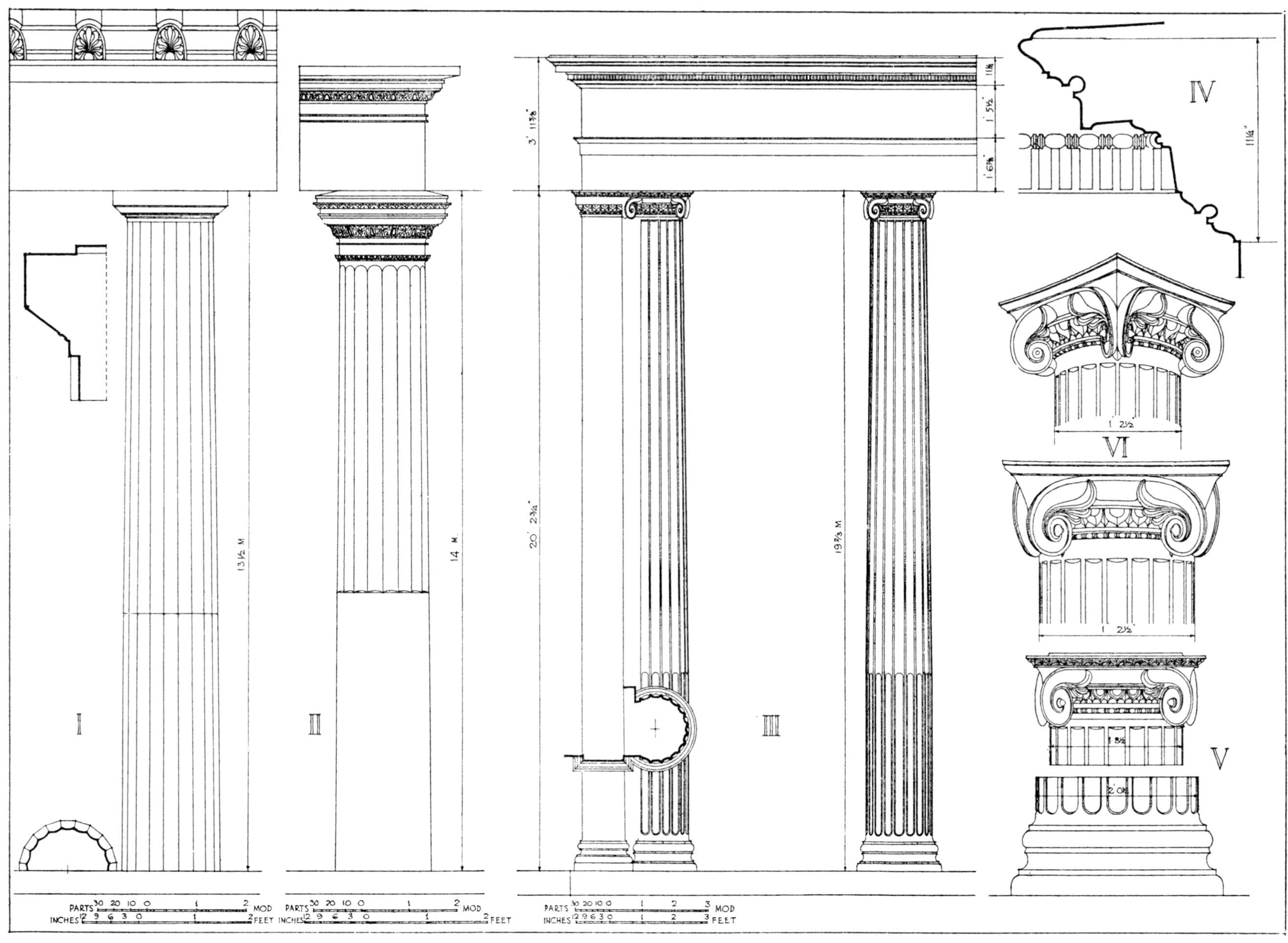

I. The "Soldiers' Quarters."
II. The "House of the Tragic Poet."

III., IV., V. The "Triangular Forum."
VI. Another Ionic Capital.

THE PORTICO OF THE PANTHEON, ROME.

THE MAISON CARRÉE, NÎMES.
ROMAN CORINTHIAN PORTICO.

(*For detail of Order see Figs.* 2 *and* 8.)

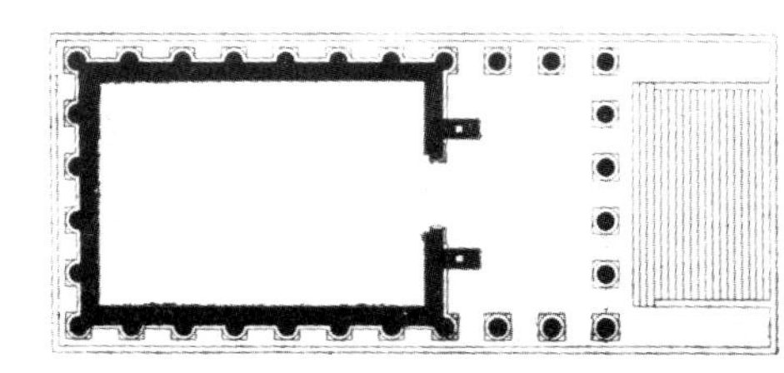

Plan Scale, Approximately 52 ft. to 1 in.

From Engravings by Clérisseau.

THE TEMPLE OF CASTOR AND POLLUX, ROME.
PERSPECTIVE DETAIL OF THE ORDER.
Coloured Drawing by an Unknown Artist of the Early Nineteenth Century in the Publishers' Collection.

THE TEMPLE OF CASTOR AND POLLUX, ROME.

DETAILS OF THE ORDER.

ROMAN COMPOSITE ORDER.

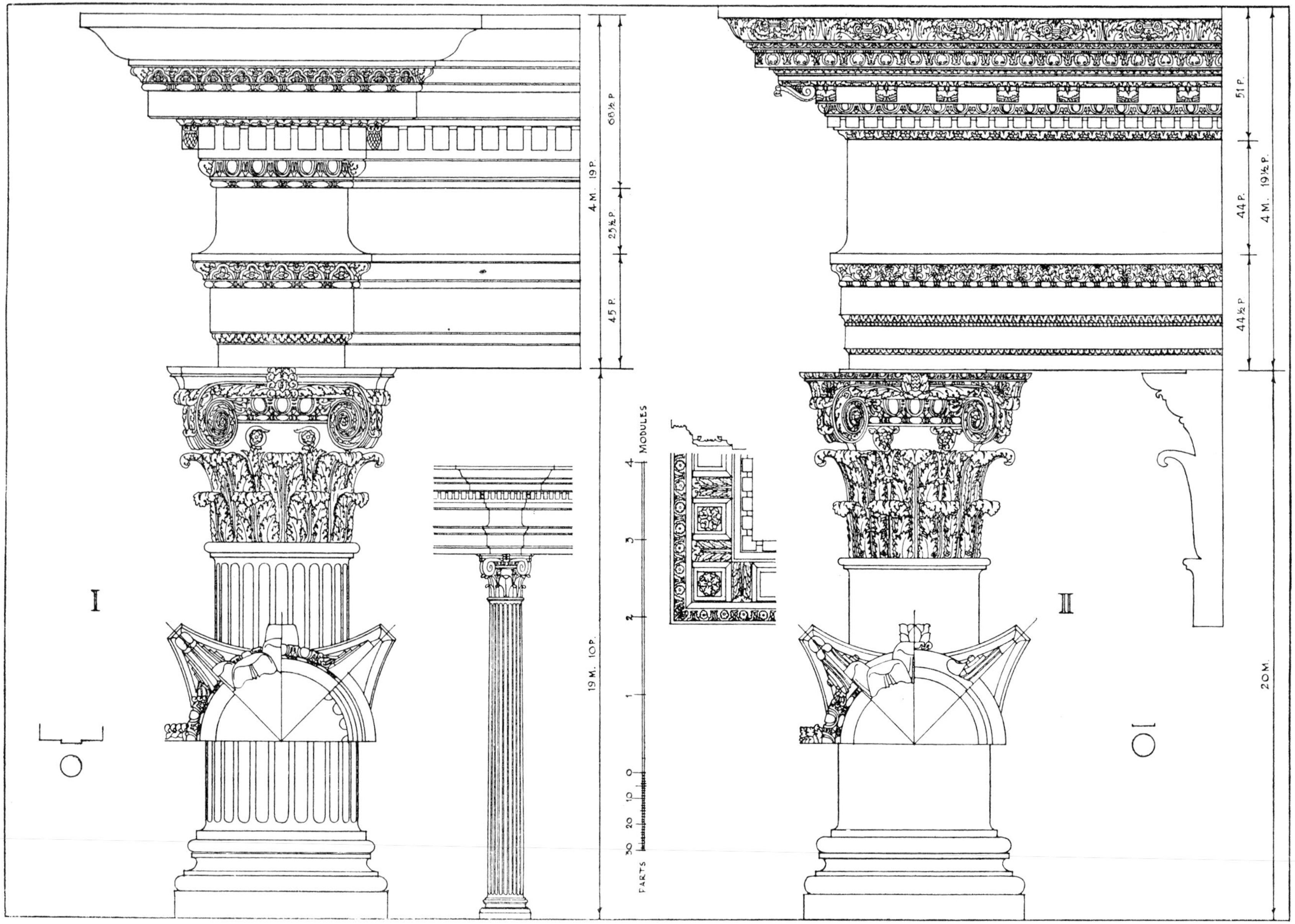

I. ORDER FROM THE TRIUMPHAL ARCH OF SEPTIMIUS SEVERUS, ROME.
See also Plate XXIII.

II. ORDER FROM THE THERMÆ OF DIOCLETIAN, ROME.

10 0 10 20 30 1 0 1 2 3 4 5 6 7 8 9 10

SCALE OF FEET SCALE OF METRES

ROMAN TRIUMPHAL ARCHES.

ARCH OF SEPTIMIUS SEVERUS, ROME. *See also Plate XXII.*

ARCH OF CONSTANTINE, ROME.

I.

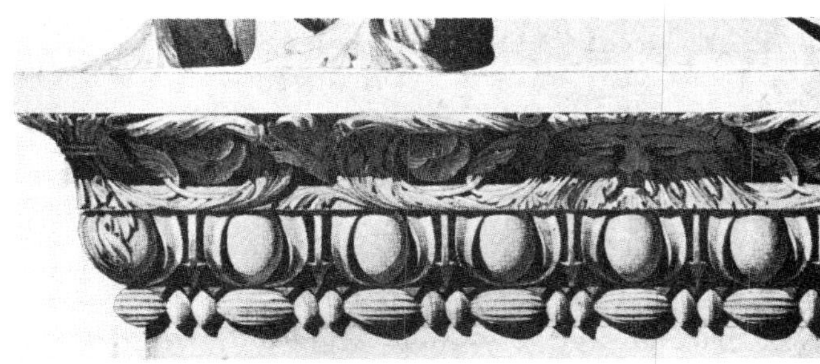

III.

II.

IV.

V.

VI.

VII.

I. & III. From the Temple of the Sun, Rome (Fragments now in the Colonna Gardens).
II. From the Forum of Trajan, Rome.
IV. From the Temple of Vespasian, Rome.
V. From the Temple of Concord, Rome.
VI. From the Column of Trajan, Rome.
VII. From the Temple of Mars the Avenger, Rome.

From Restorations edited by H. D'Espouy.

CHAPTER IV

THE ITALIAN ORDERS AND THEIR APPLICATION

If the Romans had not left behind them such a great legacy of buildings in the Classic style derived from Greece the astounding artistic development of the Renaissance could scarcely have taken place. For while it has been said that if the Classic Order had not been handed down ready-made, it would be necessary to invent it, the process of invention might have been slow and laborious.

The Renaissance in architecture naturally started in Italy, and while it may be said that it attained equally great developments elsewhere, notably

Fig. 10.—ITALIAN RENAISSANCE PILASTER CAPITALS.
From Sixteenth-Century Original Drawings.

in France and England, it was in Italy that all the thinking was done in the first instance, and here the initial steps were taken to recover and use the noble language of the Classic style. The Italians, although at first their efforts were halting, very rapidly picked up the Classic style at the stage in which the Romans left it, and displayed a remarkable mastery of its nuances. Figs. 10 and 11 show, for instance, how Italian architects contrived distinctive

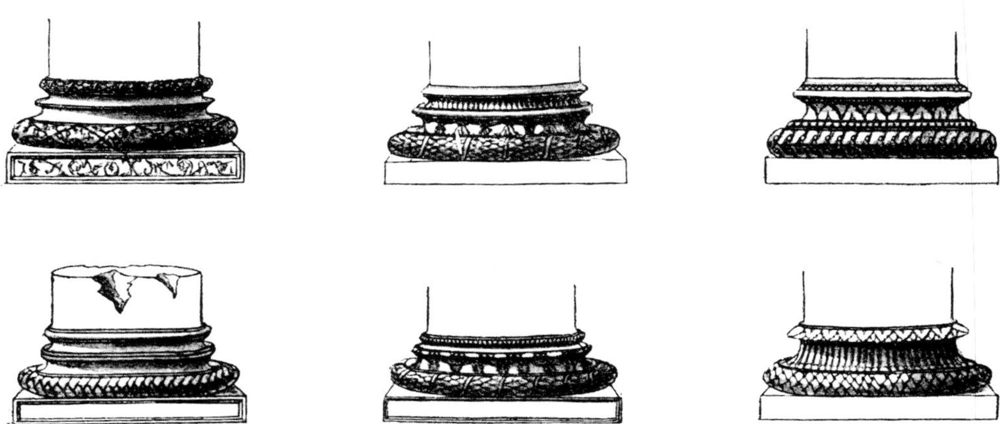

Fig. 11.—ITALIAN RENAISSANCE MOULDED AND ENRICHED BASES.
From Sixteenth-Century Original Drawings.

treatment for ornament, enriched bases, and pilaster capitals. Their native originality enabled them enormously to extend the range of Classic ornament and to discover new associations of column, arch, and vault. Yet in the writings of Vignola and Palladio a somewhat schoolmasterly attitude is noticeable, for the proportions of the Orders are set forth in dogmatic fashion without any attempt at an æsthetic justification for the proportions named. These books aimed, in the first instance, at providing rules for drawing the Orders so that the student should not allow his fancy to go astray and design associations of column and entablature without the guidance of the famous exemplars of the past.

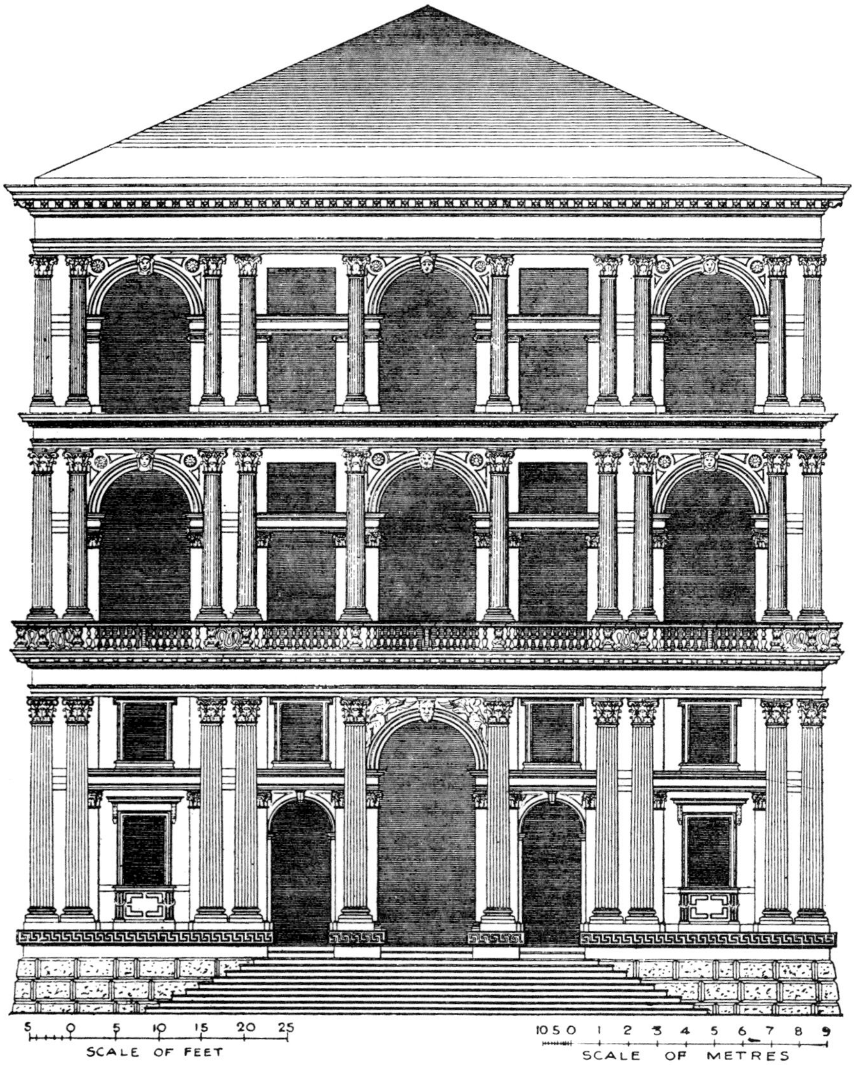

Reference has already been made to the Doric Order of Vignola, which is indeed a very beautiful rendering of the Doric style (Plates xxix.-xxxiii.), exemplifying two different types of entablature, known as the "denticular" and the "mutular" (Plate xxxiii.). The Ionic and Corinthian Orders of Vignola are also distinguished by their refinement (Plates xxxv.-xlii.). There is no doubt that it helps the student to analyse the Order and to acquire a reverence for the intellectual achievement which it represents when he is asked to take note of every feature in it and to assign to it its appropriate dimension. On the other hand, unless this type of training is supplemented by a philosophical analysis of the æsthetic function of the Order, a student will, in the last resort, revolt from this archæological interpretation, and may even decline to use the Order altogether. Such a revolt has, in fact, occurred among a large proportion of architectural students of to-day, and it can be checked only if

Fig. 12.—THE PALAZZO GRIMANI, VENICE.
Façade to the Grand Canal.
Sanmicheli, Architect.

attention is directed to the manner in which the Order solves certain ever-recurring problems of architectural design.

In the architecture of the Italian Renaissance the examples in which the columns are standing free and supporting the entablature and roof, as they do in the Greek temple, are comparatively rare. In nine instances out of ten the Order is applied to a wall which itself performs the structural function of carrying the roof, or else it is but an element of the wall surface itself, as in the pilaster formation, in which the columns are flattened out and appear to be for the most part buried in the wall. Reference to the Plates which illustrate famous Italian buildings will satisfy the inquirer on this point. In the Palazzo Grimani at Venice, by Sanmicheli (Plate LVII. and Fig. 12), the Order bears the same relationship to the arches as it does in the Roman triumphal arches, to which reference was made in the preceding chapter. Here, again, the Order provides a rectangular framework for the central arched opening. But if this be compared with the Roman example, it is apparent that the Order has been exploited still further, for in addition to the large Corinthian pilasters which support the main entablature there is a subsidiary Order which frames the smaller arches on either side, and the entablature of this second Order comes to the level of the imposts of the central arch. The three arches are united in an æsthetic relationship which cannot conceivably have been achieved by any other means. Moreover, the main Order has the effect of stabilising the vertical dimension of the façade as a whole, because as at present designed the wall cannot be stretched upwards or depressed downwards without mutilating the Order and spoiling its proportions. Again, the pilasters help to bring unity to the façade, inasmuch as they embrace two rows of openings.

Other memorable façades in which arches are related to main and subsidiary Orders are found in the Libreria Vecchia, Venice, by Sansovino (Plate LII.), the Palazzo Pesaro, Venice, by Longhena (Plate LIX.), and the Palazzo Bevilacqua, Verona, by Sanmicheli (Plate LVIII.) ; while an interesting one-storey treatment is found in the cortile of the Palazzo "Non-Finito," at Florence (Fig. 13). Often the Order is used without the arch, as in the Palazzo dei Conservatori, Rome, by Michelangelo (Plate LIII.), and here again the pilasters help to give unity to a two-storeyed building. This example is especially worthy of study because it illustrates the freedom with which the masters of the Italian Renaissance employed the Order, modifying its proportions to suit æsthetic requirements. It will be observed in this design that the entablature of the Corinthian Order is very considerably deeper than the conventional type, but this deviation from the normal was probably due to the desire of the artist to relate the entablature not only to the pilaster but to the building as a whole. While the pilasters impart a certain degree of unity to the association of ground-floor recessed opening and the windows above, this act of unification is not complete, and it appeared desirable to make the entablature and its super-incumbent balustrades so tall that it could be counted as a third storey. By this means an unresolved duality is avoided and a satisfactory trinitarian composition results. In the case of the Palazzo Valmarana, Vicenza, by Palladio (Plate LIV.), the entablature is of normal dimension, but unity is achieved by means of the attic storey, which provides a third row of windows.

In the composition of façades it is noteworthy that the pedestal beneath the columns often plays an important part. Both the ancient Romans and the Italians frequently used the pedestal, and in this respect made an advance upon the achievement of the Greeks. It is worth while to inquire into the origin of the pedestal and the æsthetic causes which are responsible for its development. The Greek column, whether Doric, Ionic, or Corinthian, was nearly always raised upon a stylobate, a short flight of steps which provided the range of columns with a suitable base. If the stylobate is removed and the columns are seen to rest upon just a plane of stone, the Order appears to be incomplete, and the columns give the impression that they are sticking barely into the ground which has been insufficiently prepared for them. It is obvious, however, that if columns can be employed only on the occasion when they can surmount a flight of steps their use would be severely restricted, and consequently some means required to be discovered whereby a column could be removed from the plane of the ground and be given a more solid punctuation at its lower extremity than is supplied by the base mouldings. This æsthetic object is fulfilled by the pedestal, and it will be observed that both Vignola and Palladio follow the example of Vitruvius and have paid great attention to the proportions of the pedestal. In fact one might almost say that the pedestal becomes a third element of the Order, almost as important as column and entablature, for it does not seem possible to vary its thickness or height except within certain well-defined limits. Obviously it could not be as tall as the column itself, because that would result in an unresolved duality. The pedestal must be considerably shorter than the column, but not so short that its separate individuality is lost and it becomes an extension of the articulated base of the column itself. It must retain its identity as a separate member in a trinitarian composition of entablature, column, and pedestal. On the other hand, it must not be of equal vertical dimension to the entablature, for this would again be a solecism, inasmuch as the functions of entablature and pedestal differ, and consequently they should not share the same vertical dimension. The width of the pedestal seems to be most logically determined when at its narrowest part it is approximately equal to the spreading base of the column. Further, it is necessary to consider that the pedestal has not only a relationship to the column but can be observed as a separate sub-unit in the composition. Therefore, it must itself have the articulation which is necessary to make it an organic whole—that is to say, it must be punctuated at its upper and lower extremities and must be free from the defect of unresolved duality. Consequently a small cornice is introduced at the top of the pedestal, and at its base a plinth, and in between these two elements is a space of blank wall sufficiently tall to dominate both cornice and plinth.

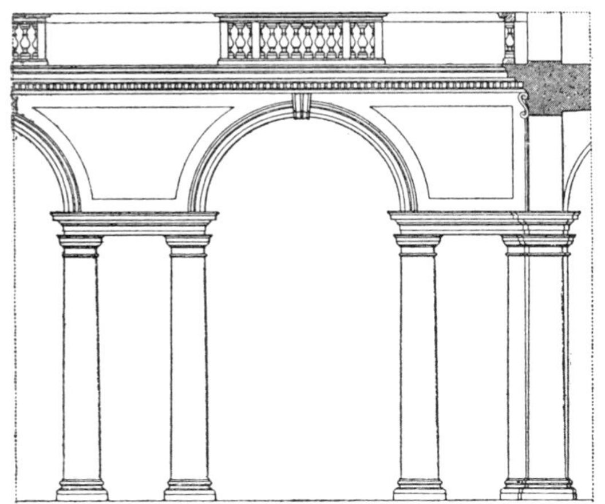

FIG. 13.—THE PALAZZO "NON-FINITO," FLORENCE.

ORDER SUPPORTING ARCHES IN THE CORTILE.

Buontalenti, Architect.

Among the ancient Romans and the Italians alike, columns between arches were almost always set up on pedestals unless there was a stylobate. In the Roman triumphal arches (Plate XXIII.) the main Order would certainly have looked rather weak if it had been carried down to the level of the ground. In Vignola's Doric Order (Plate XXXI.) both treatments are shown, one with pedestal and the other without, and the same choice is given in his treatment of the Ionic, Corinthian, and Composite Orders (Plates XXXVI., XL., and XLVI.), but he does not vouchsafe any guidance as to which treatment is to be reserved for any special architectural occasion. In the Basilica at Vicenza, by Palladio (Plate LI.), the ground-floor Order is without a pedestal, and a certain weakness results from this, although the addition of a stylobate would set matters right. This composition has the fault of unresolved duality, for Orders of comparable height are here duplicated, and there appears nothing to unify the two equal storeys. It is here interesting to observe that the Order on the first-floor storey is raised on a pedestal which is probably employed for the simple reason that it enables the Order to be harmoniously associated with a balustrade. This is another important use of the pedestal which is again exemplified in the Libreria Vecchia, Venice (Plate LII.). Obviously there is a more complete accordance between the balustrade and the Order when the balustrade happens to be on a level with a series of pedestals than when its upper member juts into the columns at an arbitrary point, as in the Queen's House, Greenwich (Plate LXX.).

Where the pedestal is made continuous, as in Plate LI., and is surmounted by two different sizes of column, there appears a certain lack of expressiveness, because one might imagine that if the pedestal is of the right proportion for the larger column it is not exactly suitable to the smaller one. In Palladio's design there is at least an element of differentiation in that the pedestal beneath the larger columns is slightly brought forward, while that of the smaller ones is in the form of a continuous parapet. In Plate LII., the Libreria Vecchia, by Sansovino, however, the pedestal is inflected beneath the columns in such a manner that those beneath the large columns, although the same height as those of the smaller, are yet broader. It is clearly not sufficient, however, that the use of the pedestal should be confined to occasions where there happens to be a balustrade, for in Plate LII. the lower extremity of the façade seems a little weak—in spite of the small stylobate which helps to punctuate it—because the upper Order, made more important by the addition of the pedestal with the balustrade, seems to have a crushing effect, and the façade is somewhat top-heavy. Here, again, is an example of the free use of the Order in which the frieze is very much increased in depth. Probably the justification of this in the mind of the artist was that the entablature of the upper Order had a double æsthetic function to perform, for it was required not only to punctuate the row of Ionic columns, but was intended to provide a crowning feature for the building as a whole. Where the entablature is artificially increased in depth for a purpose of this kind, it is the frieze which generally lends itself to expansion rather than the architrave. For it seems more important that the lower member of the entablature should have a normal relation to the columns beneath it and should be very definitely in scale with them.

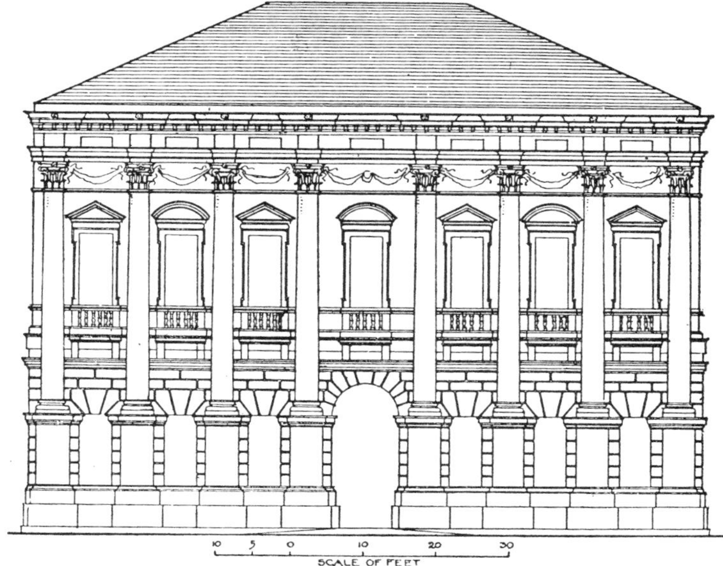

FIG. 14.—THE "CASA DEL DIAVOLO," VICENZA.
DIAGRAM OF COMPLETE FAÇADE.
Palladio, Architect.

In the superimposition of the Orders it seems especially necessary to make the ground-floor storey sufficiently solid and important-looking to dominate over the remainder, or failing this, it should be provided with a substantial plinth. Here is an instance where an understanding of the Orders themselves must be supplemented by general principles of composition. It is quite possible that if another great period of Classic architecture should arrive, as it surely must, there will be considerable new developments in the theory of superimposed Orders. It is scarcely conceivable that the Greeks themselves would have been content to place in a vertical series Orders of exactly the same type as they employed when only a single Order was used. What seems to be required here is a new type of Order which will express by its very form that it is aware of its subordination to a façade which has several rows of columns one above the other. In the Greek Order the entablature with its imposing cornice seems to be a finishing touch to a composition which is not required to proceed upwards any farther, and if it does so proceed, then the punctuation of its upper terminal ought not to be so pronounced. It is in the consideration of problems such as these that the interest of the student can once more be aroused in the Classic Order. As soon as he is given freedom to experiment in it, he will feel that the Order is a live instrument of design and no longer an exclusive possession of archæologists.

Towards the end of the Renaissance movement in Italy, during what is known as the Baroque period, considerable liberties were taken with the Orders, and in particular curved forms, both in plan and elevation, became popular, in which the entablature and pediments were bent to a number of new shapes (Fig. 15). The term Baroque is not easy to define. According to one signification, it includes almost any form of architecture which shows an original use of the Orders, but, on the other hand, its meaning is sometimes restricted to refer to certain eccentricities which assume the form of fantastic perversions of the Order without rhyme or reason. Apart from such diversions, it was quite possible for the repertory of the Classic style to be extended in many ways not thought of by the Italians, and the student of the Order will turn for enlightenment and instruction to some of the French and English exemplars such as are illustrated in the next chapter.

Fig. 15.—BAROQUE COMPOSITION BY MEISSONNIER.

CHAPTER V

FURTHER APPLICATIONS OF THE ORDERS BY ITALIAN, FRENCH, AND ENGLISH ARCHITECTS OF THE RENAISSANCE

ALTHOUGH further removed than the Italians from the main source of architectural inspiration at Rome itself, the French and English were quick to seize upon the main features of the Classic Order and to develop them in accordance with their own native genius.

Very early in its development the Classic architecture of England became associated with the street, and the buildings which best exemplify these qualities are definitely street buildings, and in a lesser degree this is true of the Renaissance architecture of France. A very large formation, such as the Louvre, Paris, with its quadrangles and long wings or terraces, represents civic design in the grand manner. The spectator is called upon to envisage a large number of windows in a single picture, and the desire to simplify the pattern of the fenestration in such a way that the multiplicity of openings does not produce an effect of monotony becomes an insistent one. It is here that the Classic Order is extraordinarily useful, for it is capable of giving an added interest and dignity to the long façade. Often it occurs that there is no practical reason for introducing a variation into window shapes ; yet the eye demands that a certain measure of order and coherence should characterise a façade studded with windows. These latter features require occasionally to be grouped, and up to now there has not been devised any system of design which groups them so intelligently and so gracefully as does the Classic Order. The reader can himself call to mind the form of terraces to be seen at Bath, and in many other English towns dating from the late seventeenth century and afterwards, in which certain parts of the long street façade are adorned with columns or pilasters in order that the terrace itself might be punctuated at its extremities or given a suitable central emphasis. Moreover, the Classic Order enables certain buildings more important than their neighbours to assume a dignity which becomes them. For instance, the very charming façade of the Society of Arts, in the Adelphi, London (Plate LXVIII.), has a degree of elaboration which would be out of place in an ordinary dwelling. There is no doubt, however, that by the employment of an Ionic Order embracing the first and second storeys, and surmounting it by a pediment, the façade immediately attracts attention to itself and achieves a great distinction of form. Occasionally the emblems of the Classic style were employed to give an architectural state to a private dwelling, but there is always a danger that the wrong kind of emphasis would result, and it would become more difficult to express the appropriate architectural distinction between public and private buildings. On Plate LXVIII. is illustrated the rear façade of a house in St James's Square, London, and it appears over-elaborate. It is, however, desirable to observe a distinction between the large and the small Order, while columns on a large scale undoubtedly enable an important public building to acquire the architectural dignity which becomes it. The very distinguished portico of University College, London (Plate LXVII.), seems entirely appropriate, while there is no need to find an excuse for the use of the Order in church buildings : the portico of the Church of St Martin-in-the-Fields (Plate LXVI.) is a singularly graceful example.

While the Order possesses a symbolic social significance which was developed more and more as the practitioners of the Classic style became more sure of themselves, there was a continuous adjustment of the parts of the Order itself, and improvements and subtleties were introduced which increased its range and expressiveness. As soon as the Order settled down to be a decorative element of wall treatment it took to itself certain qualities which previously had been associated with hewn stone arranged in courses. The rusticated columns shown on Plate LXIII. are far removed from the Greek exemplars which displayed the artist's determination at all cost to remove the signs of human labour. The ideal Greek column was a monolith, but where it was not found possible to obtain marble of the requisite size the columns were constructed of drums, the horizontal joints of which were so finely ground that they were almost invisible ; and over all—when the local material was a rough stone—the Greeks laid à very thin coat of plaster and painted the columns so that they acquired the quality of monoliths. With a rusticated wall, however, columns such as these would be out of place, and, moreover, when the column is not standing free but is definitely attached to the wall, it contributes to an architectural harmony if it shows by its very form that it was constructed by the same hands that built the wall and in the same manner. It is a tribute to the vitality of the Classic Order that even when the column or pier itself seems to be nothing more than a small, narrow strip of projecting rusticated wall, by a mere addition of capital and moulded base and the presence of an elementary entablature—or in some instances only an architrave—one immediately recognises the presence of an Order. Moreover, simplifications or elaborations of the traditional column make their appearance, and the architects of the early Renaissance in France in particular specialised in this particular development. On Plate LX., for instance, the faces of the pilasters are cut into panels, while the example from the Château d'Anet, illustrated on Plate LXI., the lower parts of the columns in the second-floor storey are elaborated and carved. It is not, however, easy successfully to introduce an additional elaboration in the drum of the column, for one of its virtues resides in its being a foil to the ornament of its capital and base. In the Archbishop's Palace at Sens (Plate LX.) the superimposition of the Orders is achieved in a most original manner, for the upper Order rests directly upon the cornice of the lower, and yet there is no undue abruptness, because the cornice of the lower entablature is projected around the base of the upper pilasters which

FIG. 16.—CHURCH OF ST CHARLES-THE-MARTYR, TUNBRIDGE WELLS, KENT.

IONIC COLUMNS AND PILASTER CAPITALS WITH ANGLE VOLUTES.

are further united to the capital of the ground-floor Order by means of a scroll which occupies the height of the frieze.

In discussing the Greek Orders it was pointed out how the Doric has an artistic advantage over the Ionic and the Corinthian, inasmuch as by means of the triglyphs the frieze is enabled to take cognizance of the position of the columns below. One cannot help asking whether it would not be possible for the cornice itself to take similar notice of the columns, and any approach to a sensitiveness of this kind is worthy of the careful attention of the designer. It is, of course, a commonplace occurrence for parapets and balustrades to have this element of expressiveness. For instance, in the example on Plate LI. the whole entablature is slightly projected over each column, and this projection is carried up to the parapet, which at these points is surmounted by statues. In the design shown on Plate LII. there is a similar treatment, except that the entablature is not projected over the columns. The frieze, however, is enabled to take account of the position of the columns, inasmuch as small openings are centrally placed above the arches. Again, in the masterful façade shown on Plate LIII. the balustrade is interrupted by a series of pedestals, the larger of which are placed exactly over the columns and thus take cognizance of their position. Moreover, the cornice in this instance is inflected by pairs of lions' heads which also are placed over the capitals. In the Palladian examples on Plate LIV. the entablatures are "returned" over both pilaster and columnar Orders.

FIG. 17.—APPLICATION OF AN ORDER IN A MONUMENTAL STAIRCASE OF THE FRENCH EMPIRE PERIOD.

One cannot say dogmatically that this treatment is superior to that in which the lines of the entablature are continuous, because it is possible to argue that the cornice loses in vigour and serenity by being interrupted in this manner, and especially is this the case when the columns are close together, as in Plate LIV. and Fig. 14. A treatment of very great interest is exemplified in Plate LIX., where it is seen that while the architrave and frieze take cognizance of the position of the columns beneath, the upper members of the cornice sweep past these interruptions, and so the building as a whole has a fine horizontal punctuation. The lower part of the cornice, however, from the

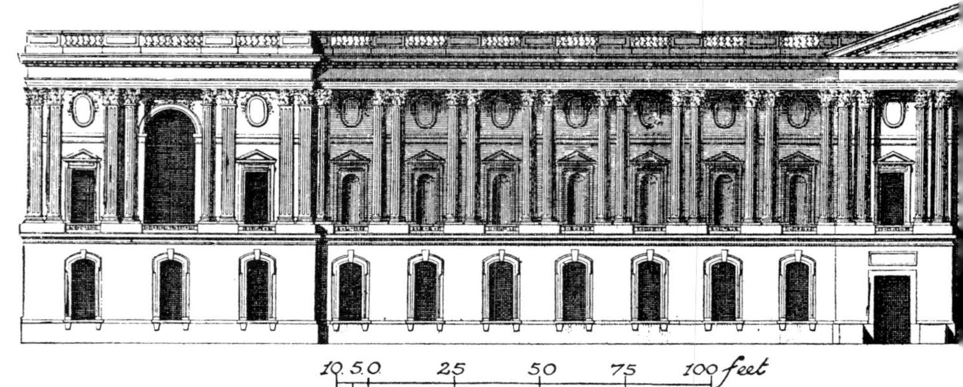

FIG. 18.—THE LOUVRE, PARI

SEE PLATE LXII. FOR DETAIL

level of the modillions downwards, expresses an inflection which enables it to unite itself to the columns below, for the sculptured heads attached to the cornice are associated with carved panels, the bases of which rest upon the projections of the architrave above the columns. This is a very subtle and distinguished design. On Plate LXII., which shows a portion of the stately east façade of the Louvre, Paris—the whole extent of which is shown in elevation in Fig. 18—the crowning balustrade is inflected to show the position of the columns, and this is also an element of expressiveness, though one cannot help feeling that the design would be more sensitive still if some part of the entablature were also inflected over the columns, for at present the capitals appear to speak to the balustrade across an area of stone which is insensitive to the presence of both.

The division of the entablature into the three elements of architrave, frieze, and cornice is so logical and so well established that comparatively few designers in the Classic style have ventured to trifle with it. Occasionally, however, the frieze and architrave have been merged into one plain fascia, as in the distinguished façade of Trinity House, London (Plate LXXI.). Here the cornice is of moderate size and its vertical dimension is considerably less than that of the remaining element of the entablature, so that the defect of unresolved duality is avoided ; for what results here is an entablature in which the cornice is really nothing more than the upper punctuation of the main member, which is the combined frieze and architrave. This very bold experiment is a complete success, and the façade shows other subtleties of composition well worthy of study. For instance, the relationship of the major and minor Orders is admirably established, for the smaller columns rest on pedestals connected with the balustrade, while their entablature — again of this simplified form — is in alignment with the moulded hoods of the window openings.

Occasionally in the much decorated style of the Brothers Adam all the members of the entablature are elaborated. An architrave at Sion House, Isleworth, for instance (Plate LXIX.), has its lower part fluted, while its upper part has not only a leaf ornament but a series of rosettes : this is a delightful composition which displays the Order in a somewhat festive mood. In positions where the structural function of the column need no longer be emphasised, the artist is free to elaborate the architrave in any way which brings it into æsthetic relationship with the other members of the entablature. The example on the same Plate, showing an entablature in Lansdowne House, London, is not quite so successful, inasmuch as the traditional enrichments on

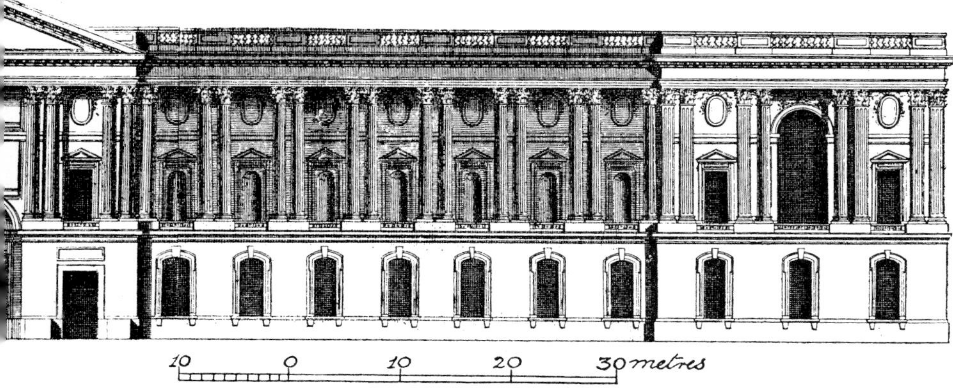

HE EAST FAÇADE.

RDER OF COUPLED COLUMNS. *Designed by Claude Perrault.*

the architrave, frieze, and cornice are not well pronounced. On Plate LXV. (iv.) a somewhat unusual design is shown in which, by virtue of its projecting foliated ornament, the frieze has the appearance of being incorporated with the cornice. This Corinthian Order from the Church of St Stephen, Walbrook, has a very small entablature, with a vertical dimension not much exceeding that of the capital itself. Probably Wren has some practical reason for doing this, but the equality between the depths of capital and entablature is not altogether happy.

An interesting development of the decoration associated with the Order occurs when the wall space underneath the architrave and immediately between the capitals is ornamented. This, too, is a form of inflection by which the wall surface appears to take cognizance of the presence of the upper terminals of the columns. In Palladio's Palazzo Tiene, Vicenza (Plate LV.), the space between the capitals is occupied by festoons, and, in fact, beneath the architrave there is what to all intents and purposes is a decorative frieze, which takes its place so harmoniously that it might almost be regarded as a subsidiary member of the entablature. Again, in his "Casa del Diavolo" at Vicenza (Plate LIV. and Fig. 14), the volutes of the capitals in the Composite Order are united by swags, as is also the case in the Palazzo Bevilacqua at Verona, by Sanmicheli (Plate LVIII. and Fig. 19). An even more illustrious example of this treatment is given on Plate LXIV., which shows one of the circular transeptal porches of St Paul's Cathedral, London, where the decorative quality of the Corinthian capitals is echoed by the wall treatment behind them.

While the Classic style has experienced such a remarkable development, one cannot help being conscious of certain fields which it has yet to conquer, and especially is it noticeable that there appears to be insufficient differentiation between exterior and interior work. Of course it may be argued that the æsthetic proportions of the Order enable it to bring the same kind of harmony to the inside of a building that it does to the outside. Yet perhaps it is not unreasonable to demand that a column should appear at first glance to be appropriate for use internally rather than for application on a street façade. Any development of the Classic style which seems to show a respect for this particular distinctiveness is worth careful consideration. A variety of elegant coved cornices have been devised which differ essentially from the exterior "dripstone" type, and the friezes associated with them have a delicacy which seems to make them especially suitable for interior decoration. In England in the latter part of the eighteenth century beautiful conventions for interior work were established, and there appeared to be a recognition that what is good enough for the exterior is not necessarily correct treatment for the interior. Sir John Soane, indeed, came to oppose the use of the Order in interior design. On the whole, however, it must be confessed that the decorative

Fig. 19.—THE PALAZZO BEVILACQUA, VERONA.

Principal Façade. *Sanmicheli, Architect.*

elements of the Classic style are so easy to employ, and they exist in such an extensive repertory, that the designer is greatly tempted to use them indiscriminately in all parts of a building.

It is difficult to imagine any style in the future which could afford to dispense with the whole range of decorative *motifs* used by the Greeks. Yet to describe these as definitely Greek is incorrect. The fret, for instance, and the scroll ornament are universal decorative forms that are to be found in the work of primitive peoples all the world over. They are not Greek, but cosmopolitan and universal. The volute, too, is an elementary form to be found both in mathematics and in nature, and it can be harmoniously associated with certain architectural elements. Nor is it likely that plant forms which have lent themselves so well to conventionalisation as do the lotus, palm, honeysuckle, and the acanthus, will be neglected by those who wish to possess a comprehensive repertory of architectural ornament. The flute, the dentil, the modillion with scroll, and the various mouldings exemplified in the Classic Order are of such simple and gracious shapes that for an artist to deny himself the privilege of using them would be a most foolish act of stultification. The egg-and-dart ornament, the bead-and-reel, the guilloche, all have their proper place and significance, and contribute to that balance which is required when elements or ornament are assembled.

There remains another quality of the Classic Order which it seems especially necessary to mention at the present time. Twentieth-century architectural innovators are frequently congratulating themselves that they have achieved what they call vertical emphasis in composition. And when this becomes slightly out of fashion it is succeeded by a rage for what is called horizontal emphasis. It may be contended that both are wrong, for both represent an exaggeration and distortion of architectural forms. It is the peculiar merit of the Classic Order that the vertical and horizontal elements are exactly balanced. The columns are strongly vertical, but the entablature and the stylobate or series of pedestals and plinth are strongly horizontal. A Greek temple is neither soaring to the heavens nor incontinently sliding sideways. It possesses the necessary architectural attribute of immobility.

* * * * *

In the foregoing pages an effort has been made to show that the Classic Order does not represent a fixed ordinance, but is something still very much alive, and if at any time it ceases to live, it will be because through sheer stupidity it has been killed, and not because it died of disease or senility. It has been said that even if the forms of the Classic Order are rejected its spirit may still survive to give animation to designs which do not even show a trace of column and entablature. It is surely, however, a fundamental error to suppose that the spirit of architecture can exist apart from its forms. For the whole object of an architectural form, the very basis of its intellectual prestige, is that it enshrines a spiritual element and constitutes the only means by which this could be manifested. The spirit of the Order can be conveyed by the Order and by no other means. The form of the Order, however, is capable of change and development : even more completely than heretofore it may serve its essential purpose of associating post and beam in organic union. For the Order is not a dead form but one which in the past has brought life to architecture, and one that will bring it still more life in the future.

A modern critic has pronounced the opinion that if a Greek of the time of Pericles were to visit an English town he would laugh heartily at seeing twentieth-century architects still employing an instrument of composition such as the Classic Order, which had originally been designed to meet the requirements of another age. Assuredly such a statement is founded upon a misapprehension of the nature of the Order, and implies the fallacy that the culture of one age must wholly obliterate that of its predecessors. It is much more likely that the Periclean Greek, if transferred to a town exemplifying some of the latest stylistic experiments, would marvel that architects could be so maladroit, blindly groping in their attempts to deal with problems of design which the Greeks, with their superior intellectual endowment, had long ago solved.

Annotated List of Plates

SECTION II

ITALIAN ORDERS AFTER VIGNOLA

Plates XXV. to XLIX. inclusive.

This series shows the five Italian Orders as standardised by Giacomo Barozzi da Vignola (1507-73), first published by him at Rome in 1563. Although many other systems have been published from time to time, notably by such Italian masters as Alberti, Palladio, Scamozzi and Serlio, and by such French and English masters as Philibert de l'Orme, James Gibbs and Sir William Chambers, it is generally accepted that Vignola embodies the best practice of the ancient Romans. In their proportions and details they present models which, if followed with discrimination, are calculated to provide a sound basis upon which to build up a knowledge of dispositions essential to the architect. They determine a high standard, but finality cannot be attained in the profiling of columns and entablatures under varying circumstances, and Vignola did not intend that his teaching should be slavishly followed. He did not, in fact, adhere closely to his own rules in the buildings which he carried out in and around Rome.

THE TUSCAN ORDER

Plates XXV. to XXVIII. inclusive.

This is the simplest of the Italian Orders and may be regarded as a rudimentary or Etruscan Doric. It is characterised by an appearance of strength, as it is plain, massive, and devoid of enriched members, while the shaft of the column is unfluted. The general sturdiness of the Order is apparent in the distyle-in-antis portico shown on Plate XXVIII., where the central intercolumniation is widened to afford clear access to the doorway. There remains no authoritative example of its use in ancient times, but it was preferred by the architects of the Renaissance in certain positions as a variation from the Doric.

The height of the column according to Vignola should be 7 Dias., or 14 Mods., and if the whole Order is divided into 5 parts, of these 4 should be given to the column and 1 or 3 Mods. 6 Pts. to the entablature, the Mod. being divided into 12 Pts. The base and capital are each 1 Mod. in height. The base consists of a square plinth with a single torus and a fillet above it, which is included in the height of the base and not in the height of the shaft as in the other Orders. The capital consists of a square abacus above an echinus, which is of quadrant section, with a single fillet, the necking beneath the bell being included in the height of the shaft. Their simplicity is apparent in the perspective sketch on Plate XXV.

The height of the entablature, which is 3 Mods. 6 Pts., is divided so that 1 Mod. is given to the architrave, 1 Mod. 2 Pts. to the frieze, which is plain, and 1 Mod. 4 Pts. to the cornice. Vignola's use of an ovolo for the topmost member of the cornice is questionable, the cyma recta being more suitable in such a position as a crowning member.

The Order used in conjunction with arches, both with and without pedestals, is shown on Plate XXVII. When used without pedestals, which is to be preferred, the columns are engaged ⅜ths of their Dia., or 9 Pts. With piers 3 Mods. wide, the width of the arched opening 6½ Mods., and the height of the opening exactly twice its width, a sufficient height of 1 Mod. is left for the keystone.

When the column is set upon a pedestal, the total height should be divided into 19 parts: then, 4 of these will be given to the pedestal, 3 to the entablature, and the remaining 12 will give the height of the column, which, divided into 14 parts, as before, will give the Module. The columns are engaged ⅓rd of their diameter, or 8 Pts. With a pier 4 Mods. wide, and the arched opening 8 Mods. 9 Pts. wide, and a height exactly twice its width, it allows of a simple archivolt 1 Mod. wide, which leaves sufficient space between it and the soffit of the architrave. The perspective sketches show the relation of the Order to the piers and arches.

Details of the pedestal, which, however, is rarely used with this Order, are included on Plate XXVI. Vignola made it ⅓rd the height of the column, or 4 Mods. 8 Pts., including a simple base and capping, each of which is ½ Mod., or 6 Pts., in height. The width of the die of the pedestal is 2 Mods. 9 Pts., which is the same as that of the plinth of the base. Archivolts and imposts suitable for use with this Order are given on the same Plate.

THE DORIC ORDER

Plates XXIX. to XXXIII. inclusive.

This Order also expresses strength and is characterised by the austerity of its several parts. The column, according to Vignola, should be 8 Dias., or 16 Mods. high, including the capital and base, and the shaft is generally fluted with twenty shallow flutes, meeting at an arris. If the total height of the Order is divided into 5 parts, 4 of these are given to the column and 1 to the entablature, and if divided into 20 parts the module is obtained, which is divided into 12 parts, as with the Tuscan Order. The base is 1 Mod. high, with a torus, astragal, and fillet, and the capital is also 1 Mod. high, exclusive of the necking. It has more members than the Tuscan capital and is lighter in effect. The entablature is 4 Mods. high, and of these 1 Mod. is given to the architrave, 1½ Mods. to the frieze, and 1½ Mods. to the cornice. Triglyphs occur in the frieze, and these, contrary to Greek practice, are always placed over the axes of columns even at external angles, as shown in the perspective sketch on Plate XXX. The triglyphs are 1 Mod. wide, and the metopes being square are 1½ Mods. wide. The spacing of the triglyphs governs the intercolumniation, which must allow for a definite number of square metopes, as seen in the tetrastyle portico shown on Plate XXIX. The bed-mould of the cornice permits of two distinct treatments, the one with a dentil band which distinguishes the *denticular* Doric Order, and the other with mutules placed over every triglyph, which characterises the *mutular* Doric Order. In both, the soffit of the corona is panelled, but the mutular is the less severe of the two and permits of carved enrichments on the capital. Comparative perspective sketches of the angles of the denticular and mutular Orders are given on Plate XXXIII.

The Order used in conjunction with arches, both with and without pedestals, is shown on Plate XXXI. In both cases the columns are engaged not more than ⅓rd of their diameter, so that the projection of the impost at the springing of the arch shall not protrude in an unsightly manner beyond the axis of the column. If there are no pedestals, with piers 3 Mods. wide and the arched opening 7 Mods. wide, an exact spacing of triglyphs and metopes is obtained in the frieze. The height of the arched opening is preferably twice its width and this allows of an archivolt of sufficient width, with the necking of the shaft continued from column to column, as Vignola preferred.

When pedestals are used the total height should be divided into 25⅓rd parts, and one of these will give the Mod. The column being always 16 Mods. high and the entablature 4 Mods. high, the pedestal will be 5⅓rd Mods. high, which is ⅓rd of the height of the column. With piers 5 Mods. wide and the opening 10 Mods. wide, an exact spacing of metopes and triglyphs is obtained in the frieze. The width of the pedestal is the same as that of the plinth of the base of the column, or 2 Mods. 10 Pts., and it has a base 10 Pts. high and a capping 6 Pts. high, as shown on Plate XXXII., where suitable archivolts and impost mouldings are also given.

PEDIMENTS USED WITH THE TUSCAN AND DORIC ORDERS

Plate XXXIV.

Methods of determining the height of pediments suitable for use with the Tuscan and Doric Orders are given on this Plate. The lack of uniformity in the inclination of pediments in ancient examples led Serlio to formulate this simple procedure.

Draw a horizontal line level with the top of the cornice, and from the point where it intersects the centre line of the pediment, with the greatest projection of the cornice as a radius, describe an arc cutting the centre line. From the point so obtained, describe another arc with the distance to the same point of the cornice as a radius, and its intersection with the centre line will determine the height of the pediment.

It should be noted that in the *denticular* Doric Order the dentils in the sloping cornice are vertical, and in the *mutular* Doric the mutules have vertical sides immediately over those in the horizontal cornice beneath.

THE IONIC ORDER

Plates XXXV. to XXXVIII. inclusive.

This Order is more graceful than the preceding ones, and by the increase in the relative height of its column, the slenderness of its mass, and the elegance of its capital, it attains a quality intermediate between the grave solidity of the Doric and the exuberant richness of the Corinthian.

The height of the column is increased to 9 Dias., or 18 Mods., including the capital and base, and the Mod. is divided into 18 Pts., because the detail of the Order is more delicate than in the Tuscan and Doric Orders. The shaft is fluted with 24 semicircular flutes separated by fillets, which should be about $\frac{2}{7}$ths of the width of the flutes, and they are shown stopping square above the apophyge of the base, but with semicircular ends under the capital. The base of the column is 1 Mod. high, exclusive of the top fillet, and in its design Vignola substituted several small members for the lower torus of the Attic base, which is ordinarily used with this Order. The capital is very distinctive, and a method of setting out its volutes is given on Plate XXXVIII. If the total height of the Order is divided into 5 parts, 4 of these are given to the column and 1, or $4\frac{1}{2}$ Mods., to the entablature; of these $1\frac{1}{4}$th Mods. are given to the architrave, $1\frac{1}{2}$ Mods. to the frieze, and $1\frac{3}{4}$ths Mods. to the cornice. The architrave is divided into 3 plain faces crowned by an enriched member: the frieze may be an unbroken face or enriched with carving in relief, and the cornice has bed-mouldings which are enriched.

The Order used in conjunction with arches, both with and without pedestals, is shown on Plate XXXVI. The columns are engaged $\frac{1}{3}$rd Mod. in the pier. When there are no pedestals, the pier may be 3 Mods. wide, and the opening is shown $8\frac{1}{2}$ Mods. wide and exactly twice its width in height, which allows of a suitable archivolt. When the columns are placed on pedestals, the whole height should be divided into $28\frac{1}{2}$ parts, 1 of which gives the Mod., 18 the height of column, and $4\frac{1}{2}$ that of the entablature as before, the remaining 6 parts determining the height of the pedestal. The piers are 4 Mods. wide and the opening 11 Mods., with a height of 22 Mods., which allows of an architrave and keystone. The pedestal has the same width as that of the plinth of the base, or 2 Mods. 14 Pts., and its base and capping are each 9 Pts. high (Plate XXXVII.).

A method of drawing the volute of the capital is given on Plate XXXVIII. In Fig. ii. draw the *cathetus*, a vertical line 1 Mod. from the axis of the column, and intersect with a horizontal line from the top of the astragal 12 Pts. below the top of the abacus. The point so obtained will be the centre of the eye of the volute, which is circular and about 2 Pts. in dia. In this circle, which is enlarged in Fig. iii., draw a square as shown, and divide each half-diagonal into 3 parts. This gives 12 points to be used as centres for the 12 arcs which comprise the spiral of the complete volute. With point 1 as centre, and as a radius the vertical distance to the horizontal line defining the extent of the volute, draw the first arc terminating at the horizontal line 1, 2; then take point 2 as centre, with the extremity of the arc already described as radius, and draw an arc terminating at the vertical line 2, 3. Repeat this operation with each of the remaining points of the 12, and the curve of the outer edge of the volute will be obtained. To draw the inner curve, subdivide each of the 3 divisions of the diagonals (Fig. iii.) into 4 equal parts, and from each division nearest to the point already used as a centre describe 12 other arcs.

The sides of the capitals at right angles to the volute faces are known as the "bolsters," or "cushions," and their various contours are best drawn by hand.

At an external angle the volute is placed diagonally (Plate XXXVII.), so that the capital may be well balanced on both faces. There is precedent in both Greek and Roman Orders for this solution of the difficult problem of treating the Ionic capital at an external angle.

The Order shown on Plate XXXVIII., i., with 4 angle volutes, is after Scamozzi, as Vignola does not give any example of this useful variety in which all four faces of the capital are identical, there being no "cushions." The Attic base is preferable with this capital, and it may be enriched as shown, with the flutes terminating both top and bottom with semicircular ends.

THE CORINTHIAN ORDER

Plates XXXIX. to XLII. inclusive.

This Order is characterised not only by its more slender proportions but also by the increased richness of its capital and entablature. The height of the column is 20 Mods., or 10 Dias., and that of the entablature 5 Mods., or ⅕th that of the whole Order, which, if divided into 25 parts, will give the Mod. As with the Ionic Order, the Mod. is divided into 18 Pts. The shaft of the column has 24 semicircular flutes divided by fillets. Of the 5 Mods. given to the entablature, 3 are divided equally between the architrave and the frieze, and the remaining 2 give the height of the cornice, which is distinguished by its modillions ; these should be so spaced that one always occurs over the axis of a column.

The Order used in conjunction with arches, both with and without pedestals, is shown on Plate XL. The columns are engaged ⅓rd Mod. in the pier. When there are no pedestals the pier may be 3 Mods. wide and the opening 9 Mods. wide, and twice its width in height. When the columns are placed on pedestals the whole height should be divided into 32 parts, and of these 20 will be given to the column and 5 to the entablature as before, the remaining 7 parts giving the height of the pedestal, which is rather more than ⅓rd the height of the column. The piers being 4 Mods. wide and the opening 12 Mods. wide and 25 Mods. high allows of satisfactory spacing of the modillions, and sufficient depth for the keystone, but it departs from Vignola's rule of making the height of the opening exactly twice its width. The pedestal has a width of 2 Mods. 14 Pts., which is the same as that of the plinth of the base : the die is 2 squares high and a base of 12 Pts., and capping of 14 Pts. make up the total height of 7 Mods. Details of the pedestal, and of archivolts and keystone suitable for use with the Order, are given on Plate XLI.

The " bell " of the capital is strongly marked, and the arrangement of acanthus leaves, angle volutes, and intermediate caulicoli beneath the concave-sided abacus is shown on Plate XLII. The differences between the column capital and the pilaster capital are only such as are necessitated by the change from the circular to the rectangular plan.

PEDIMENT USED WITH THE CORINTHIAN ORDER

Plate XLIII.

The method of determining the height of pediments given on Plate XXXIV. applies also to pediments used with the other Orders. The detail of a Corinthian pediment given on this Plate is especially to explain the relation of the modillions and dentils on the sloping cornice to those on the horizontal cornice.

THE PROFILING OF THE SHAFTS OF COLUMNS

Plate XLIV.

I. Method of Setting-out Profile of Shaft diminishing from ⅓rd Height of Shaft

Having decided height and top and bottom dia. of shaft, draw a semicircle at ⅓rd of total height from the base. Divide one-quarter of this semicircle and the remaining two-thirds of shaft into the same number of equal parts. Vertical lines drawn from divisions of the semicircle to corresponding divisions of shaft (as shown on the Plate), will give points through which the profile is drawn. Measure from centre line for profile of other side.

II. Method of Setting-out Profile of Shaft diminishing whole Height of Shaft

Having set out height and top and bottom dia. of shaft, draw a horizontal line through base of shaft and continue indefinitely. From extreme point of top half diameter, set off distance of half-bottom diameter, upon the axis. Starting from extreme point of top dia., draw a line through point obtained upon the axis, and continue until it cuts the indefinite line. From this point of intersection draw through axis of column any number of lines. On each of these lines, from axis to circumference, set off distance of half bottom dia. A curve drawn through the points thus obtained will give the profile.

III. Method of Setting-out Wreathed Shaft

Having set out height and top and bottom dia. for wreathed shaft, draw alongside a diminished column of same height and diameter (method No. II. on this Plate serves the purpose). Draw a small cylinder below wreathed column and upon its axis. The dia. of this circle will determine the amount of twist to be given to the profile of shaft. Divide the circle into 8 equal parts, and from the points obtained upon its circumference project 5 vertical lines (one will be the axis). Divide the shaft and that of diminished column into 48 equal parts. Draw central spiral; the points 1, 2, 3, and 4 in lower and the upper 4 parts of the 48 are obtained from the cylinder (see diagram), the rest are at intersections of vertical and horizontal lines. The wreathed profile is obtained by setting-out the corresponding diameter of diminished column, line for line, and using the intersections of the spiral as centres.

THE COMPOSITE ORDER

Plates XLV. to XLVIII. inclusive.

The relative proportions of column and entablature and their various parts are similar to those of the Corinthian Order. The principal differences consist in the design of the capital and the greater elaboration of the entablature, the Order permitting of a profuse use of moulded and carved enrichment. The capital, however, is the distinctive feature, and it consists of an Ionic capital with 4 angle volutes placed above two ranges of acanthus leaves similar to those used with the Corinthian Order. Details of column and pilaster capitals are given on Plate XLVIII.

Plate XLIX.

Vignola's Orders are here shown in perspective with the entablatures "returned" over coupled columns and pilasters.

THE TUSCAN ORDER, WITH PERSPECTIVE OF ANGLE.

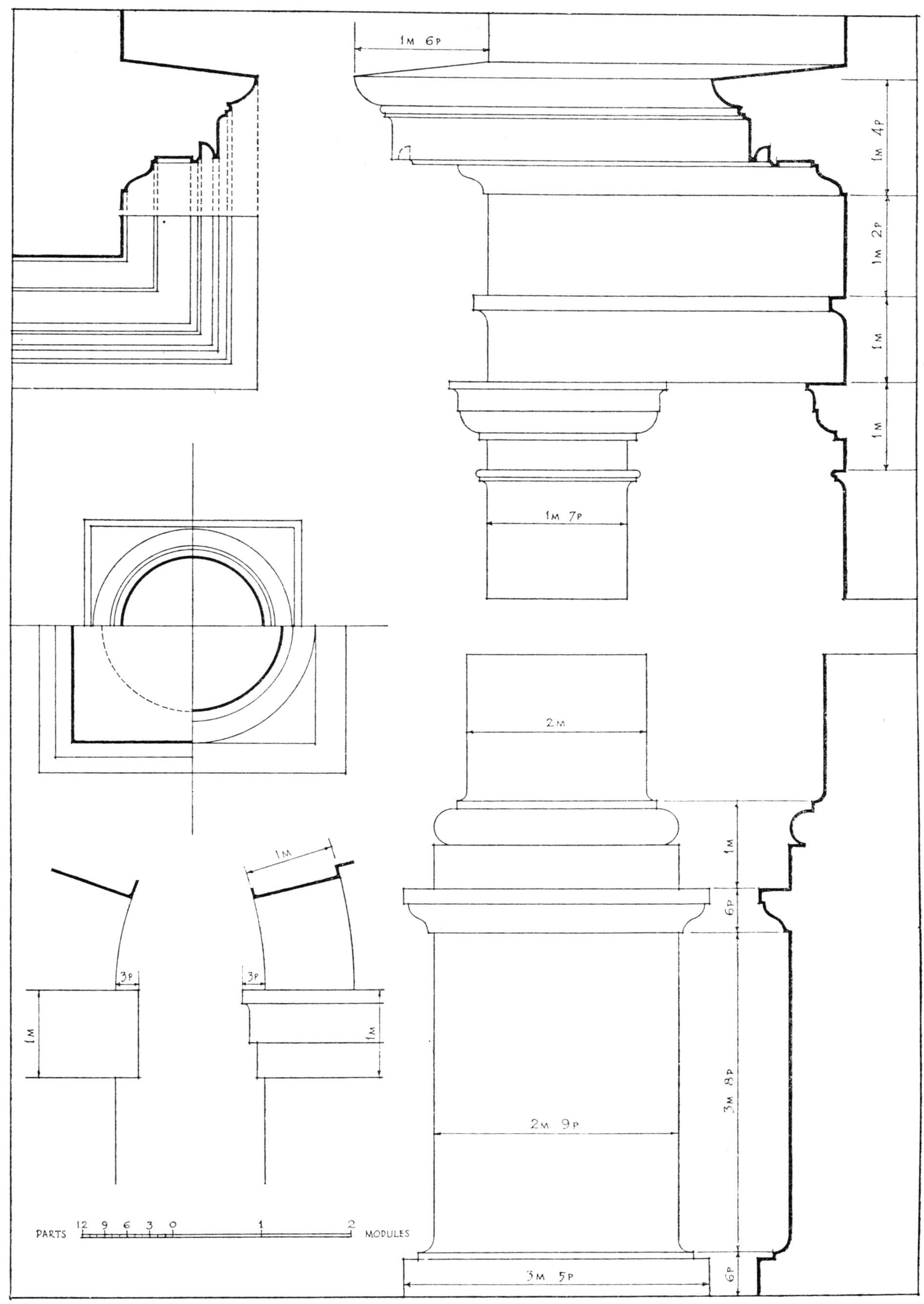

DETAIL OF THE ORDER WITH PEDESTAL.

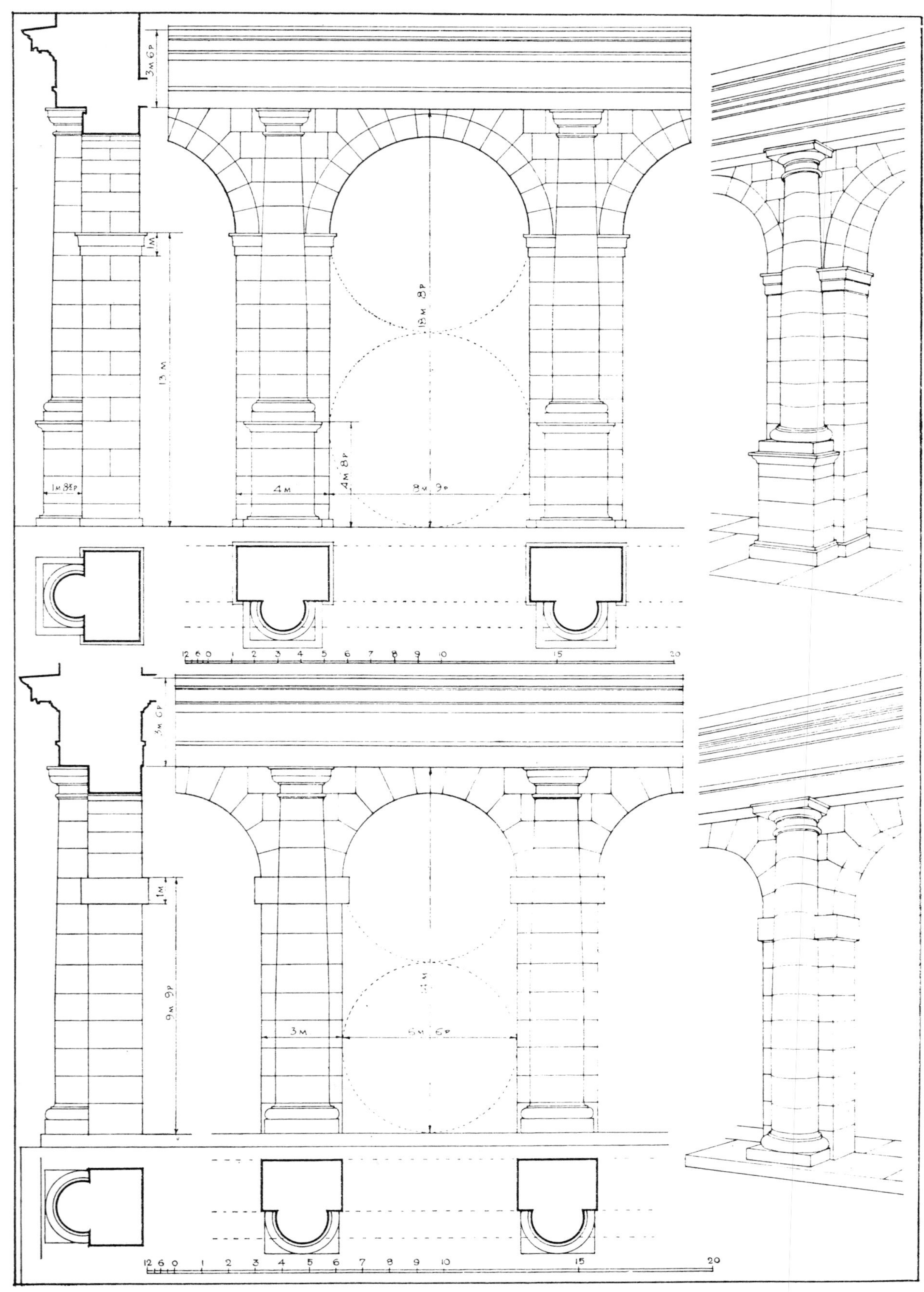

THE ORDER WITH AND WITHOUT PEDESTALS USED WITH ARCHES.

DISTYLE-IN-ANTIS PORTICO.

A TETRASTYLE PORTICO.

THE DENTICULAR DORIC ORDER, WITH PERSPECTIVE OF ANGLE.

THE DENTICULAR ORDER, WITH AND WITHOUT PEDESTALS USED WITH ARCHES.

DETAIL OF THE DENTICULAR ORDER, WITH PEDESTAL.

I. Detail of the Mutular Order.
II. Perspective of the Angle of the Denticular Order shown on Plates XXX. and XXXII.
III. Perspective of the Angle of the Mutular Order shown on this Plate.

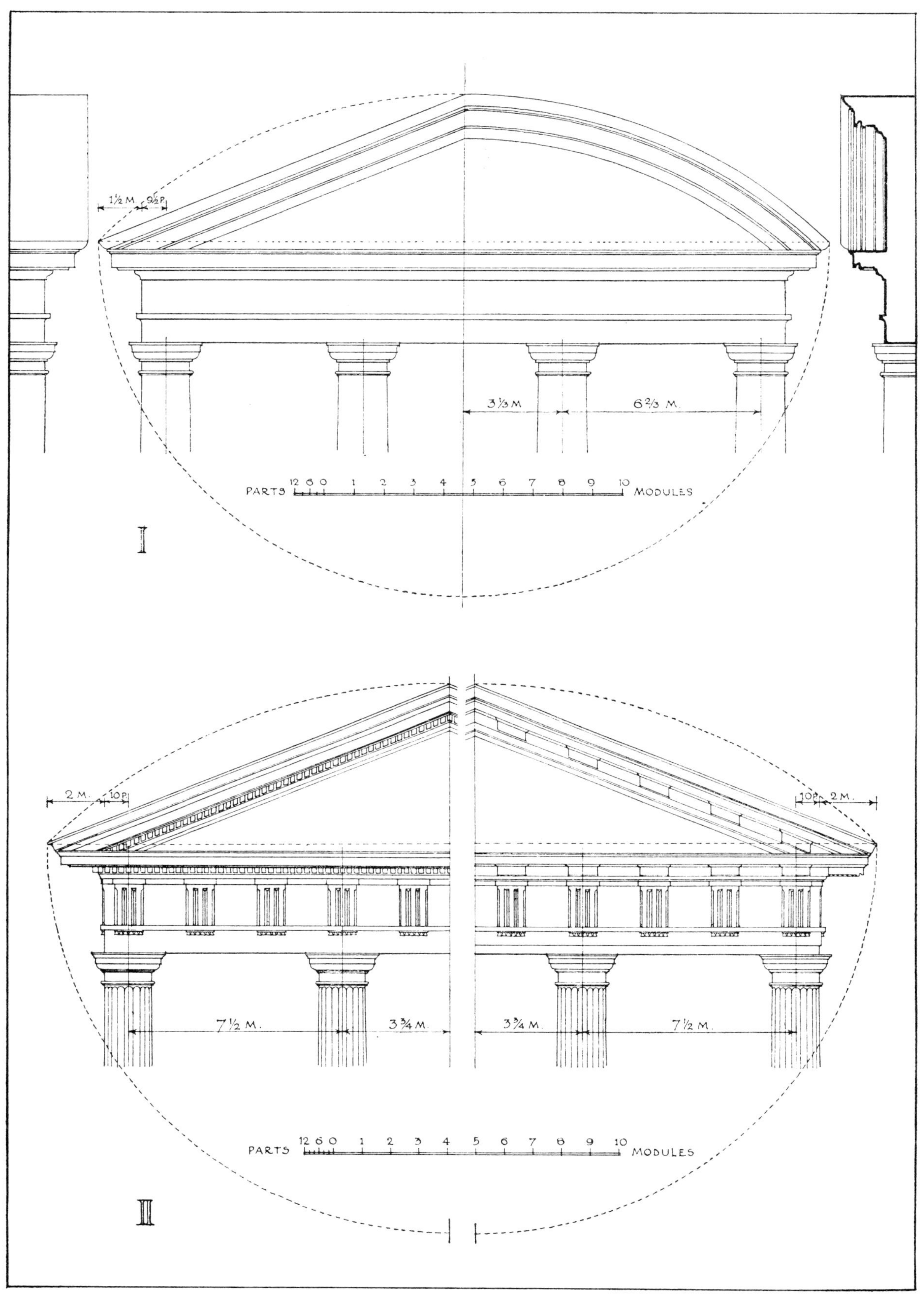

I. Setting-out of Straight and Curved Pediments used with the Tuscan Order.
II. Setting-out of Pediments used with the Denticular and Mutular Doric Orders.

THE IONIC ORDER, WITH PERSPECTIVE OF ANGLE.

THE ORDER WITH AND WITHOUT PEDESTALS USED WITH ARCHES.

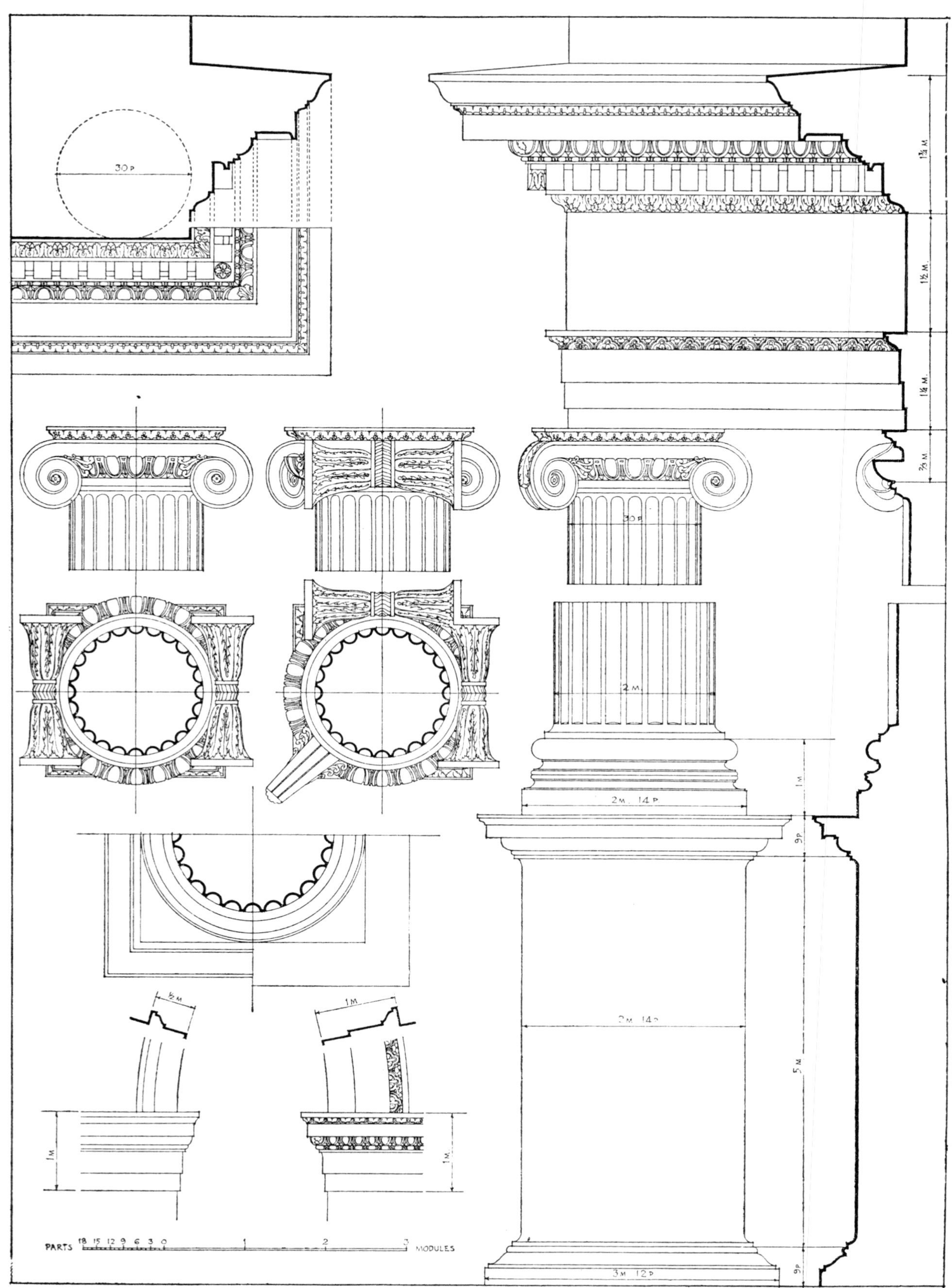

DETAIL OF THE ORDER WITH PEDESTAL.

Ionic Orders of Scamozzi and Vignola.

Plate XXXVIII.

I. Ionic Order with Four Angle Volutes, after Scamozzi.
II. Detail of Ionic Capital of Vignola's Order.
III. Enlargement of Eye of Volute, showing Setting-out of Centres for Describing Volutes.

THE CORINTHIAN ORDER, WITH PERSPECTIVE OF ANGLE.

THE ORDER WITH AND WITHOUT PEDESTALS USED WITH ARCHES.

DETAIL OF THE ORDER WITH PEDESTAL.

CORINTHIAN ORDER OF VIGNOLA.

PLATE XLII.

DETAIL OF PILASTER AND COLUMN CAPITALS.

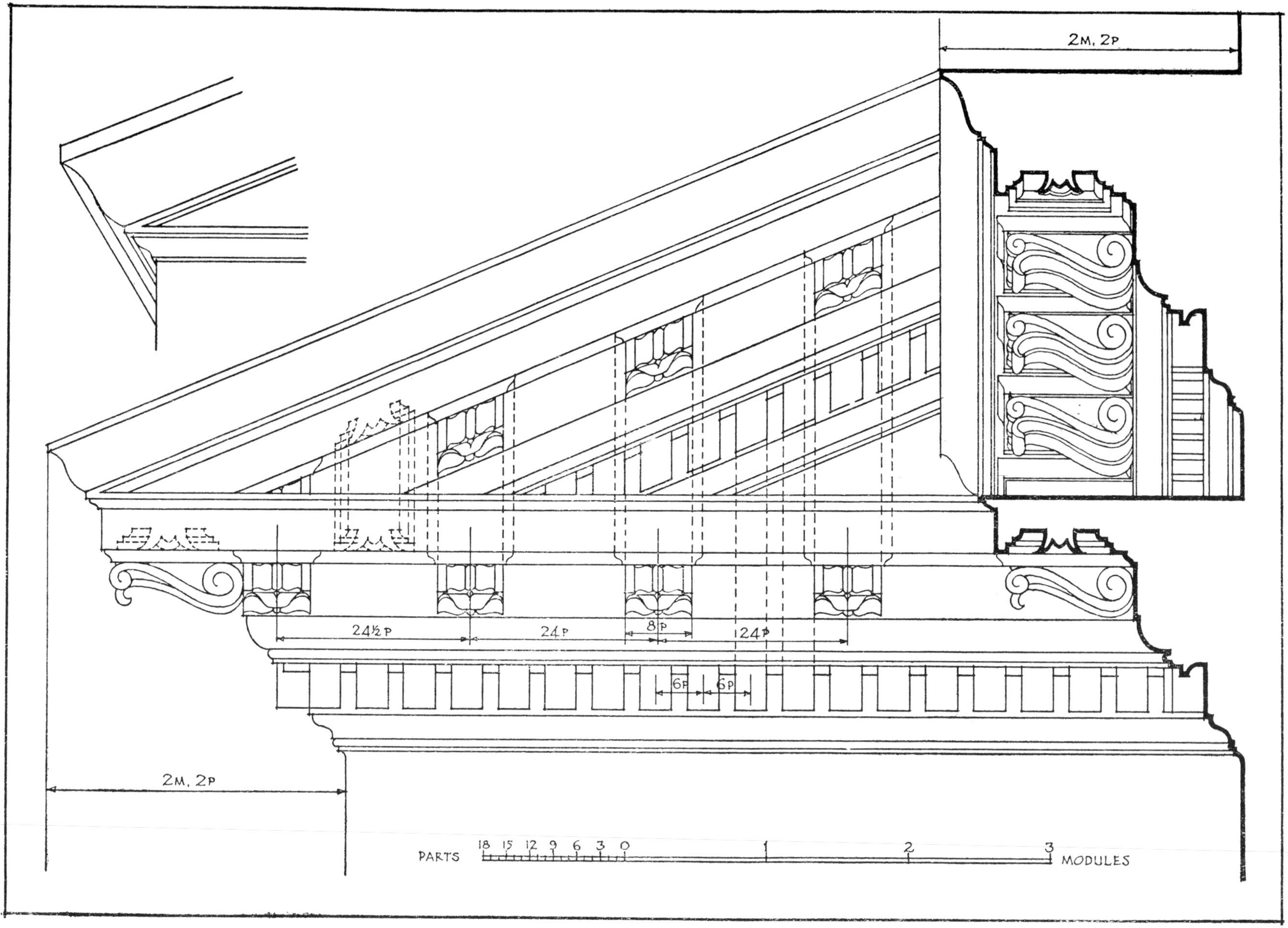

2M, 2P

24½P

24P

8P

24P

6P

6P

2M, 2P

PARTS 18 15 12 9 6 3 0 1 2 3 MODULES

DETAIL OF ANGLE OF PEDIMENT, SHOWING SETTING-OUT OF MODILLIONS.

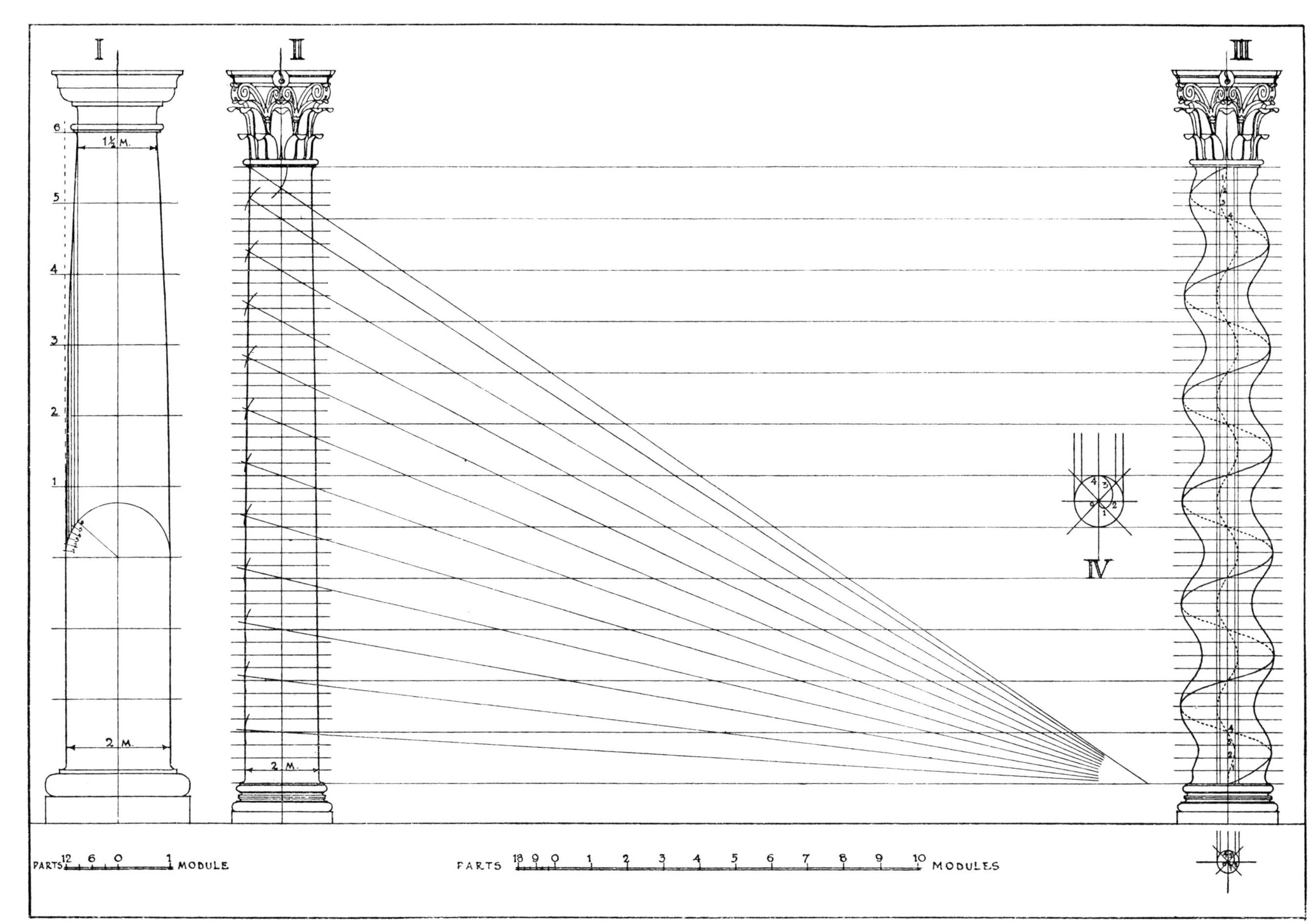

I. Method of Setting-out Profile of Shaft Diminishing from One-third Height of Shaft.
II. Method of Setting-out Profile of Shaft Diminishing Whole Height of Shaft.
III. Method of Setting-out Wreathed Shaft.
IV. Enlargement of Cylinder used in Setting-out Central Spiral of Wreathed Shaft.

THE COMPOSITE ORDER, WITH PERSPECTIVE OF ANGLE.

THE ORDER WITH AND WITHOUT PEDESTALS USED WITH ARCHES.

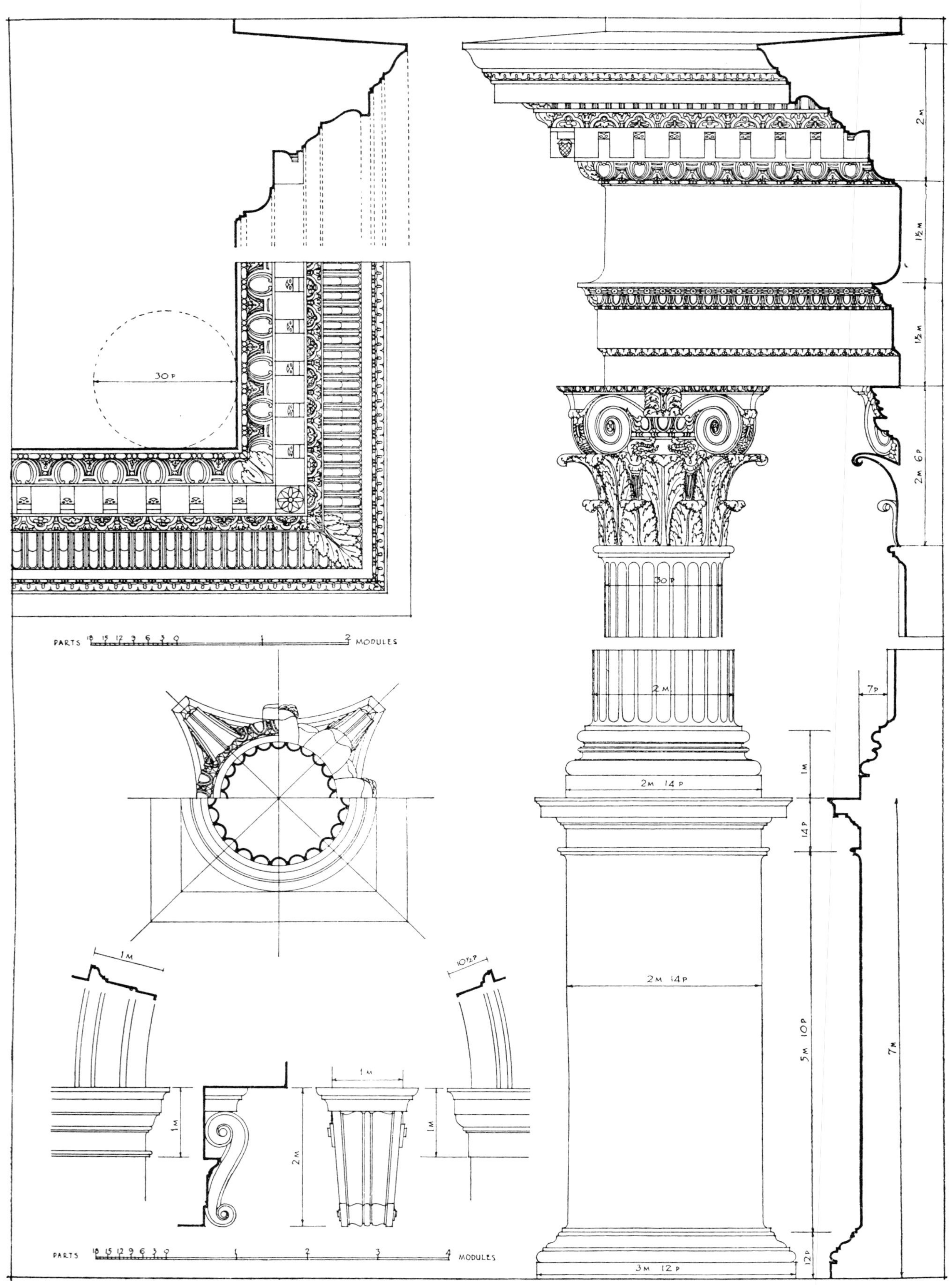

DETAIL OF THE ORDER WITH PEDESTAL.

DETAIL OF PILASTER AND COLUMN CAPITALS.

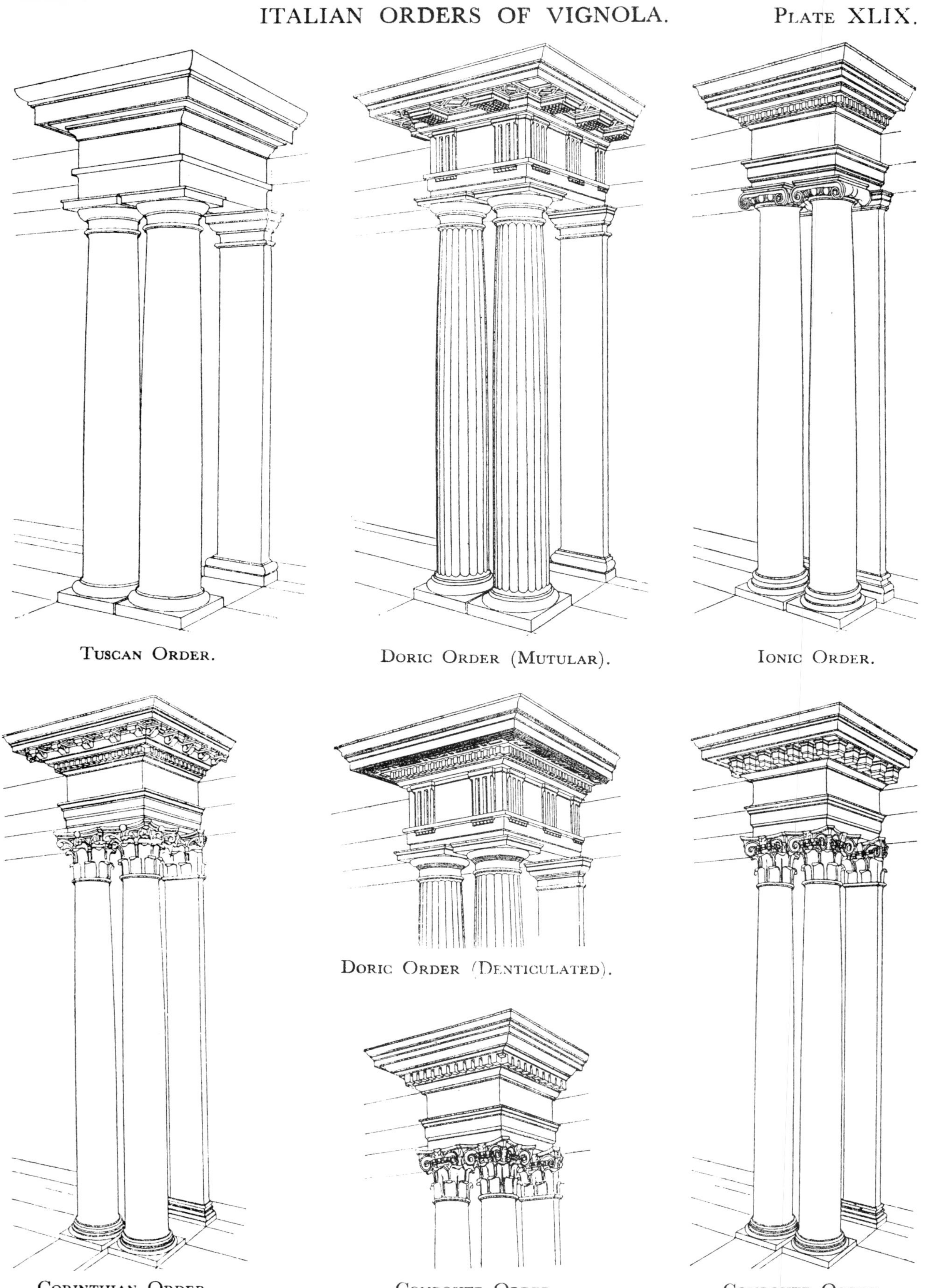

TUSCAN ORDER.

DORIC ORDER (MUTULAR).

IONIC ORDER.

DORIC ORDER (DENTICULATED).

CORINTHIAN ORDER.

COMPOSITE ORDER.

COMPOSITE ORDER.

THE ITALIAN ORDERS ACCORDING TO VIGNOLA, WITH ENTABLATURES "RETURNED" OVER COUPLED COLUMNS AND PILASTERS.

Annotated List of Plates

SECTION III

APPLICATION OF THE ORDERS

ITALIAN RENAISSANCE BUILDINGS

Plate L.—THE PALAZZO DELLA GRAN GUARDIA VECCHIA, VERONA, 1609. Domenico Curtoni, architect. End elevation. Rusticated lower storey; upper storey, coupled attached Doric columns surmounted by mutular entablature. Height, 72 ft. to top of cornice.

Plate LI.—THE "BASILICA," VICENZA, 1549. Andrea Palladio, architect. Part elevation, and section showing the "Motif Palladio" used with Doric and Ionic Orders superimposed. The arcading was constructed of stone by Palladio around the old Gothic Consiglio. Entablature broken over each column. Height, 62 ft. to top of upper balustrading.

Plate LII.—THE LIBRERIA VECCHIA, VENICE, 1536. Jacopo Sansovino, architect. Part elevation, section and plan showing Ionic Order above arcaded lower storey of the Doric Order. Height, 51 ft. to top of upper cornice. Built of Istrian stone.

Plate LIII.—THE PALAZZO DEI CONSERVATORI, ROME, 1564-68. Michelangelo, architect. Part elevation and plan of the façade. The Corinthian Order in pilaster form is carried through two storeys. This building forms part of Michelangelo's lay-out of the top of the Capitoline Hill. Façade, 66 ft. high.

Plate LIV.—*Left*, THE PALAZZO VALMARANA, VICENZA, 1556. Andrea Palladio, architect. Part elevation of façade showing Composite Pilaster Order carried through two storeys. Secondary Corinthian Order to lower storey. Façade, 49 ft. to top of cornice.

Right, THE "CASA DEL DIAVOLO," VICENZA, 1570. Andrea Palladio, architect. Known also as the "Antica Posta." Part elevation showing Composite Order. Three-quarter engaged columns are raised on high pedestals which reach to top of ground-floor windows. Only two bays were built out of the seven comprising the whole façade (Fig. 12). Façade, 60 ft. high.

Plate LV.—*Left*, THE PALAZZO POMPEII, VERONA, 1530. Michele Sanmicheli, architect. Part of principal façade. Doric Order on high pedestals above a rusticated lower storey. Height, 44 ft. to top of cornice.

Right, THE PALAZZO TIENE, VICENZA, A.D. 1536. Andrea Palladio, architect. Part of principal façade. Composite Order above a rusticated lower storey.

Plate LVI.—THE CHURCH OF SANTA MARIA DELLE CARCERI, PRATO, 1485-91. Guiliano da San Gallo, architect. Greek cross plan, the arms wagon-vaulted over the pilaster Order given on right of the Plate. The Order of coupled pilasters of the exterior is given on the left of the Plate.

Plate LVII.—THE PALAZZO GRIMANI, VENICE, 1549. Michele Sanmicheli, architect. The façade has three storeys of superimposed Orders in pilaster form (Fig. 10); the Corinthian Order of the lowermost storey is illustrated on this Plate. Façade, 97 ft. high.

Plate LVIII.—THE PALAZZO BEVILACQUA, VERONA, 1527. Michele Sanmicheli, architect. Part elevation and plan, showing attached Corinthian Order above a rusticated Doric Order, Upper columns raised on high pedestals above balustrade, and some of the shafts fluted spirally (Fig. 17).

Plate LIX.—THE PALAZZO PESARO, VENICE, 1679. Baldassare Longhena, architect. A design which exhibits the excess of detail characteristic of the Baroque exuberance of the time. Three-storeyed façade. The Plate shows plan and elevation of the Composite Order with detached columns of the second storey.

FRENCH RENAISSANCE BUILDINGS

Plate LX.—THE ARCHBISHOP'S PALACE, SENS, 1535-37. One bay of the Henry II. wing. Example of Gothic freedom applied to Roman design, incorporating classical elements introduced from Italy.

Plate LXI.—CHÂTEAU D'ANET, NORMANDY, 1548-54. Philibert de l'Orme, architect. Elevation, section, and details of central feature of one of the principal façades. Three storeys of superimposed Orders.

Plate LXII.—THE LOUVRE, PARIS. Part of the east façade, 1667-74. Claude Perrault, architect. This façade is 600 ft. in length ; the basement storey serves as a podium for colonnades of coupled Corinthian columns, between side wings and a pedimented centre-piece (Fig. 16).

BANDED AND RUSTICATED ORDERS

Plate LXIII.

I. FRENCH. BANDED ORDER, DORIC. Philibert de l'Orme, architect.

II. FRENCH. BANDED ORDER, IONIC. Philibert de l'Orme, architect.

III. FRENCH. RUSTICATED ORDER. Hôtel de Montescot, Chartres, *c.* 1610.

IV. FRENCH. RUSTICATED ORDER. Château de Tanlay, 1643-48. Le Muet, architect.

V. FRENCH. RUSTICATED PILASTER ORDER. Château de Sully, 1567-96. Charles Ribonnier, architect.

VI. ITALIAN. RUSTICATED DORIC ORDER. Palazzo Rezzonico, Venice, 1650. Baldassare Longhena, architect.

VII. ITALIAN. RUSTICATED DORIC ORDER. Porta Nuova, Verona, 1541. Michele Sanmicheli, architect.

VIII. ENGLISH. RUSTICATED DORIC ORDER. Seaton Delaval, Northumberland, 1720. Sir John Vanbrugh, architect.

IX. and X. ENGLISH. RUSTICATED ORDERS WITH SQUARE BLOCKS. Palladian. Sir William Chambers, architect.

ENGLISH RENAISSANCE BUILDINGS

ORDERS FROM SIR CHRISTOPHER WREN'S CITY CHURCHES

Plate LXIV.—ST PAUL'S CATHEDRAL, LONDON, 1675-1710. Sir Christopher Wren, architect. Plan and elevation of North Transept Porch. Semicircular projecting porch with entablature supported on four free and two attached Corinthian columns. Columns, 40 ft. high ; dia. 4 ft., with "cabled" fluting.

Plate LXV.

I. CHURCH OF ST BRIDE, FLEET STREET, 1680. Capital, plan, and entablature of coupled Doric columns of nave arcades.

II. CHURCH OF ST AUGUSTINE, WATLING STREET, 1683. Ionic Order of nave columns.

III. THE CHURCH OF ST JAMES, GARLICK HITHE, 1682. Capital and entablature of Ionic Order of nave columns.

IV. THE CHURCH OF ST STEPHEN, WALBROOK, 1672-79. Interior Corinthian Order of sixteen columns, eight of which carry a central dome.

V. THE CHURCH OF ST MARTIN, LUDGATE HILL, 1684. Capital and entablature of Interior Composite Order.

VI. THE CHURCH OF ST ANNE AND ST AGNES, ALDERSGATE, 1681. Capital and entablature of Interior Corinthian Order.

Plate LXVI.—THE CHURCH OF ST MARTIN-IN-THE-FIELDS, LONDON, 1722. James Gibbs, architect. Corinthian hexastyle portico at west front, with flanking pilasters of same Order. This dignified entrance portico is surmounted by a pediment and raised on a stylobate of several steps.

Plate LXVII.—THE PORTICO OF UNIVERSITY COLLEGE, LONDON, 1827-29. William Wilkins, architect. Built in the time of the Greek revival, this is one of the finest Classical porticoes in England. Twelve Corinthian columns (ten in front) are raised high above an original and impressive arrangement of steps and podium.

ORDERS FROM THE WORKS OF ROBERT AND JAMES ADAM

Plate LXVIII.—*Left*, THE SOCIETY OF ARTS, JOHN STREET, ADEPLHI, LONDON, 1772-74. Front elevation, with upper storey façade of Ionic Order and central "Venetian" window.

Right, THE HOUSE OF SIR WATKYNS WILLIAMS WYNNE, 20 ST JAMES'S SQUARE, LONDON, 1773. Robert Adam, architect. Elevation of rear block to courtyard. Rusticated basement storey and upper storey with similar *motif* to that used on the façade of the Society of Arts.

Plate LXIX.—*Left*, SION HOUSE, ISLEWORTH, MIDDLESEX, 1761-62. Robert Adam, architect. Ionic Order of the ante-room, and cornice and base of attic over entablature.

Right, LANSDOWNE HOUSE (formerly Shelburne House), BERKELEY SQUARE, LONDON, 1765. Robert Adam, architect. Ornate Order, with capital based on that of the "Tower of the Winds," Athens (Plate XIII.). Entablature of doorway of the dining-room.

Plate LXX.—*Above*, THE INCORPORATED LAW SOCIETY BUILDING, CHANCERY LANE, LONDON, 1830-36. Centre part of façade, from a drawing by Lewis Vulliamy, the architect of the original building. One of his early works and a design strongly influenced by the Greek revival.

Below, THE QUEEN'S HOUSE, GREENWICH, 1617-35. Inigo Jones, architect. Drawing by Lewis Vulliamy of centre part of façade. One of the earliest examples of pure Palladian exterior design in English domestic building.

Plate LXXI.—TRINITY HOUSE, TOWER HILL, LONDON, 1793-98. Samuel Wyatt, architect. Principal façade, with centre slightly recessed. Over a rusticated lower storey, principal and secondary Ionic Orders are skilfully adjusted to solids and voids respectively, and to one another.

Plate LXXII.—THE BANK OF ENGLAND, LONDON, 1795-1827. Sir John Soane, architect. View in the Lothbury courtyard : part of Soane's remodelling of the old building and a fine example of the Græco-Roman phase. Order founded on that of the Temple of Vesta at Tivoli.

Plate LXXIII.—*Left*, PRESTON HALL, MIDLOTHIAN, *c.* 1800. Robert Mitchell, architect. View of wing as seen from within the drawing-room. From a drawing by Mitchell, 1802.

Right, SOMERSET HOUSE, LONDON, 1776-86. Sir William Chambers, architect. Gateway at end of North Terrace. Example of Roman Palladian phase, with rusticated Doric Pilaster Order.

ORDERS FROM AMERICAN COLONIAL BUILDINGS

Plate LXXIV.—ENTRANCE PORCH, TUCKER HOUSE, SALEM, MASSACHUSETTS, 1808. Application of free Classic details and motives of the Georgian phase in England. Details of slender Composite Order of wood construction.

Plate LXXV.—ENTRANCE PORCH IN DUMBARTON AVENUE, COLUMBIA, U.S.A., *c.* 1810. A free rendering of the Classic Order, with slender columns 8 ft. 5 ins. high. Entablature and pediment of wood, with appropriate detail.

DOORWAYS, WINDOWS, AND BALUSTRADES

GREEK DOORWAY

Plate LXXVI.—NORTH DOORWAY OF THE ERECHTHEUM, ATHENS. (See also notes on Plate VI.) Height of opening, 17 ft. 2 ins. ; width, 8 ft. 1½ ins. at foot ; 7 ft. 6¾ ins. at top ; thus showing a diminution usual in Greek doorways.

ROMAN DOORWAY

Plate LXXVII.—PANTHEON, ROME. (See also notes on Plate XIX.) The doors—the finest and most ancient in Rome—are of bronze, as are also the side pilasters and the grille over. Height of opening, 38 ft. 11 ins. ; height of doors, 24 ft. 2 ins.

ITALIAN RENAISSANCE DOORWAYS

Plate LXXVIII.

I. THE PALAZZO CANCELLARIA, ROME : considered to have been built by Bramante, 1495-1505. Design for a doorway by Vignola which, however, was not executed.

II. THE PALAZZO ALBERGATI, BOLOGNA, 1521-40. Baldassare Peruzzi, architect. The principal entrance doorway in stone on a brick façade.

ITALIAN RENAISSANCE WINDOWS

Plate LXXIX.

I. The Palazzo Farnese, Rome, 1534. Antonio da San Gallo, architect. Top storey and cornice added by Michelangelo, 1546. Design for first-floor window by San Gallo ; the pediments are alternately triangular and segmental.

II. The Palazzo Albergati, Bologna, 1521-40. Baldassare Peruzzi, architect. Detail of first-floor window over centre doorway, for which see Plate LXXIX.

BALUSTRADES

Plate LXXX.

I., II. and III. From The "Castle" of Caprarola, 1547-49. Vignola, architect.

IV. From The Palazzo Lante, Rome, 1520. Baldassare Peruzzi, architect.

V. From The Palazzo Farnese, Rome. Antonio da San Gallo, architect.

VI. From The Vatican, Rome. Bramante, architect. Cortile of San Damaso, 1503-13. Balustrade to second storey.

VII. From The Vatican, Rome. Bramante, architect. Cortile of San Damaso, 1503-13. Balustrade to first storey.

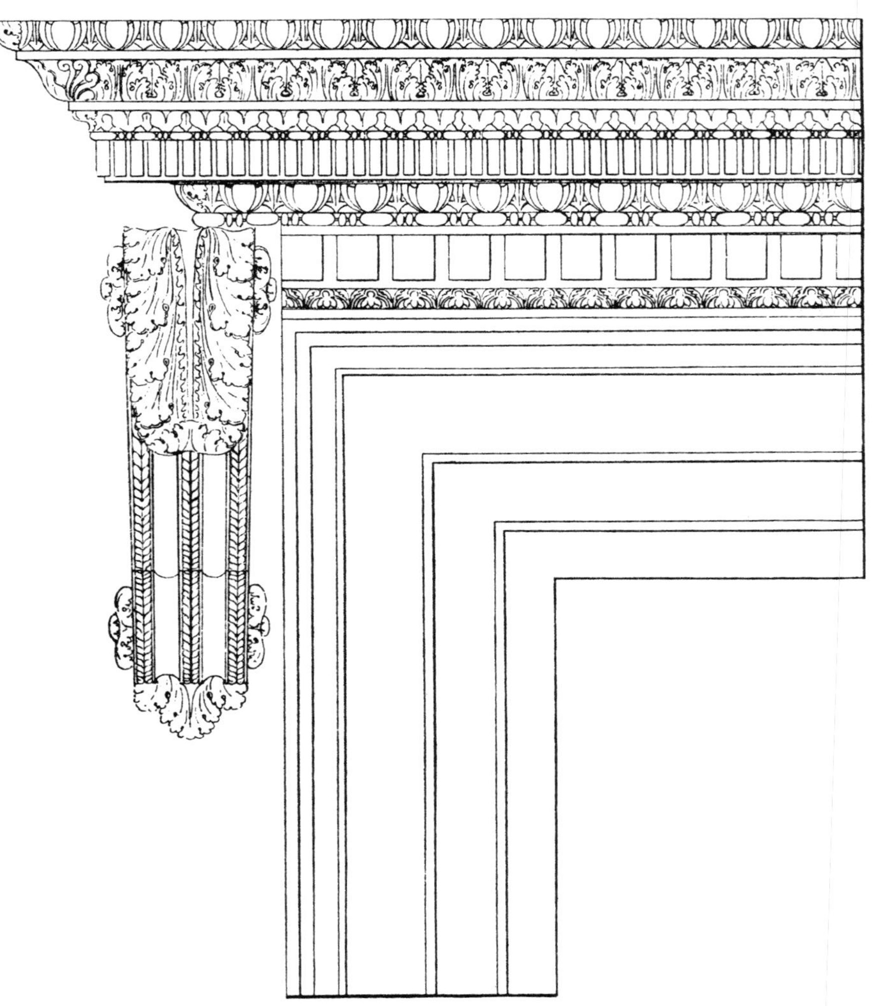

Fig. 20.—THE MAISON CARRÉE, NÎMES.
Detail from Doorway.

PART OF THE PALAZZO DELLA GRAN GUARDIA VECCHIA, VERONA.

SHOWING THE MUTULAR DORIC ORDER USED ABOVE A RUSTICATED LOWER STOREY.

Domenico Curtoni, Architect.

THE "BASILICA," VICENZA.

THE "MOTIF PALLADIO" USED WITH DORIC AND IONIC ORDERS SUPERIMPOSED.

Palladio, Architect.

THE LIBRERIA VECCHIA, VENICE.

Jacopo Sansovino, Architect.

THE PALAZZO DEI CONSERVATORI OF THE CAPITOL, ROME.
CORINTHIAN ORDER CARRIED THROUGH TWO STOREYS.

Michelangelo, Architect.

THE PALAZZO VALMARANA, VICENZA.
Composite Pilaster Order with Secondary Corinthian Order to Lower Storey.
Palladio, Architect.

THE "CASA DEL DIAVOLO," VICENZA.
Composite Order on High Pedestals.
Palladio, Architect.

PART OF THE PALAZZO POMPEII, VERONA.
DORIC ORDER ABOVE A RUSTICATED LOWER STOREY.
Sanmicheli, Architect.

PART OF THE PALAZZO TIENE, VICENZA.
COMPOSITE ORDER ABOVE A RUSTICATED LOWER STOREY.
Palladio, Architect.

THE CHURCH OF SANTA MARIA DELLE CARCERI, PRATO.

Guiliano da San Gallo, Architect.

THE PALAZZO GRIMANI, VENICE.

THE LOWER STOREY, WITH CORINTHIAN ORDERS.

Sanmicheli, Architect.

PART OF THE PALAZZO BEVILACQUA, VERONA.
CORINTHIAN ORDER ABOVE A RUSTICATED DORIC ORDER. *Sanmicheli, Architect.*

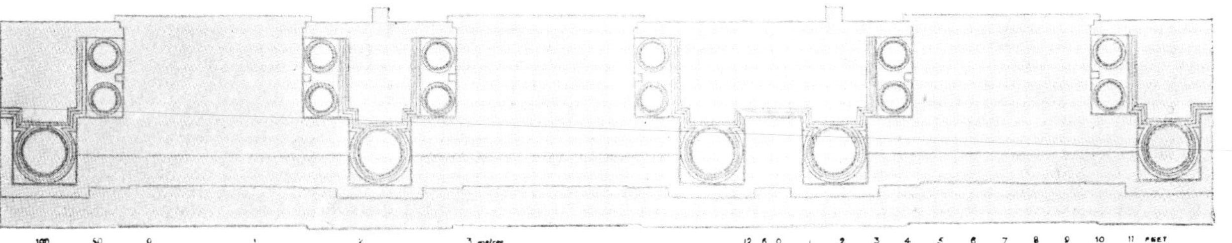

THE PALAZZO PESARO, VENICE.

THE SECOND STOREY, WITH COMPOSITE ORDERS.

Baldassare Longhena, Architect.

THE ARCHBISHOP'S PALACE, SENS.

BAY OF THE HENRY II. WING.

FRAGMENT OF THE CHÂTEAU D'ANET.

Philibert de L'Orme, Architect.

THE LOUVRE, PARIS.
PART OF THE EAST FAÇADE.

Designed by Claude Perrault.

BANDED AND RUSTICATED ORDERS.

FRENCH.

I. BANDED DORIC ORDER. *Philibert de L'Orme, Architect.*
II. BANDED IONIC ORDER. *Philibert de L'Orme, Architect.*
III. RUSTICATED ORDER, HOTEL DE MONTESCOT, CHARTRES.
IV. RUSTICATED ORDER, CHÂTEAU DE TANLAY. *Le Muet, Architect.*
V. RUSTICATED PILASTER ORDER, CHÂTEAU DE SULLY. *Ribonnier, Architect.*

ITALIAN.

VI. RUSTICATED DORIC ORDER, PALAZZO REZZONICO, VENICE. *Longhena, Architect.*
VII. RUSTICATED DORIC ORDER, PORTA NUOVA, VERONA. *Sanmicheli, Architect.*

ENGLISH.

VIII. RUSTICATED DORIC ORDER, SEATON DELAVAL, NORTHUMBERLAND. *Sir John Vanbrugh, Architect.*
IX., X. RUSTICATED ORDERS, WITH SQUARE BLOCKS. *Sir William Chambers, Architect.*

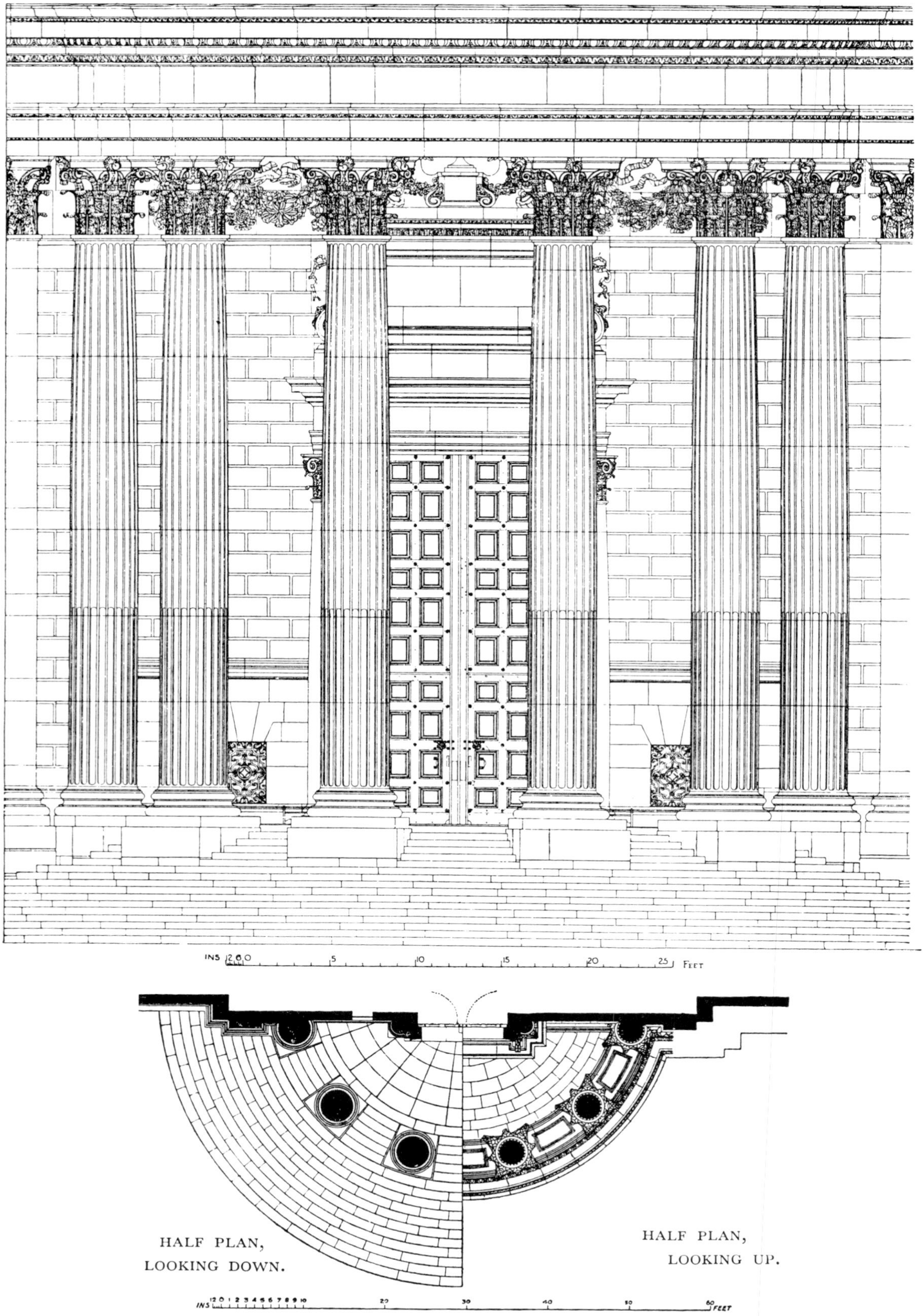

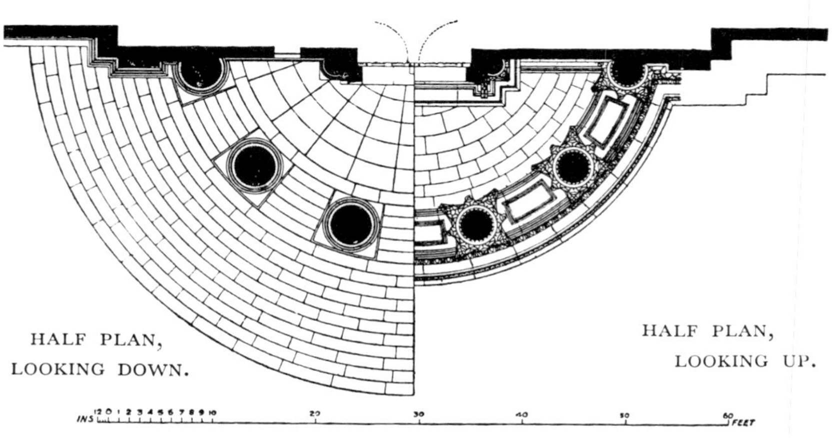

ST PAUL'S CATHEDRAL, LONDON.

THE CORINTHIAN ORDER OF THE NORTH PORCH.

From Measured Drawings by Robert S. Weir.

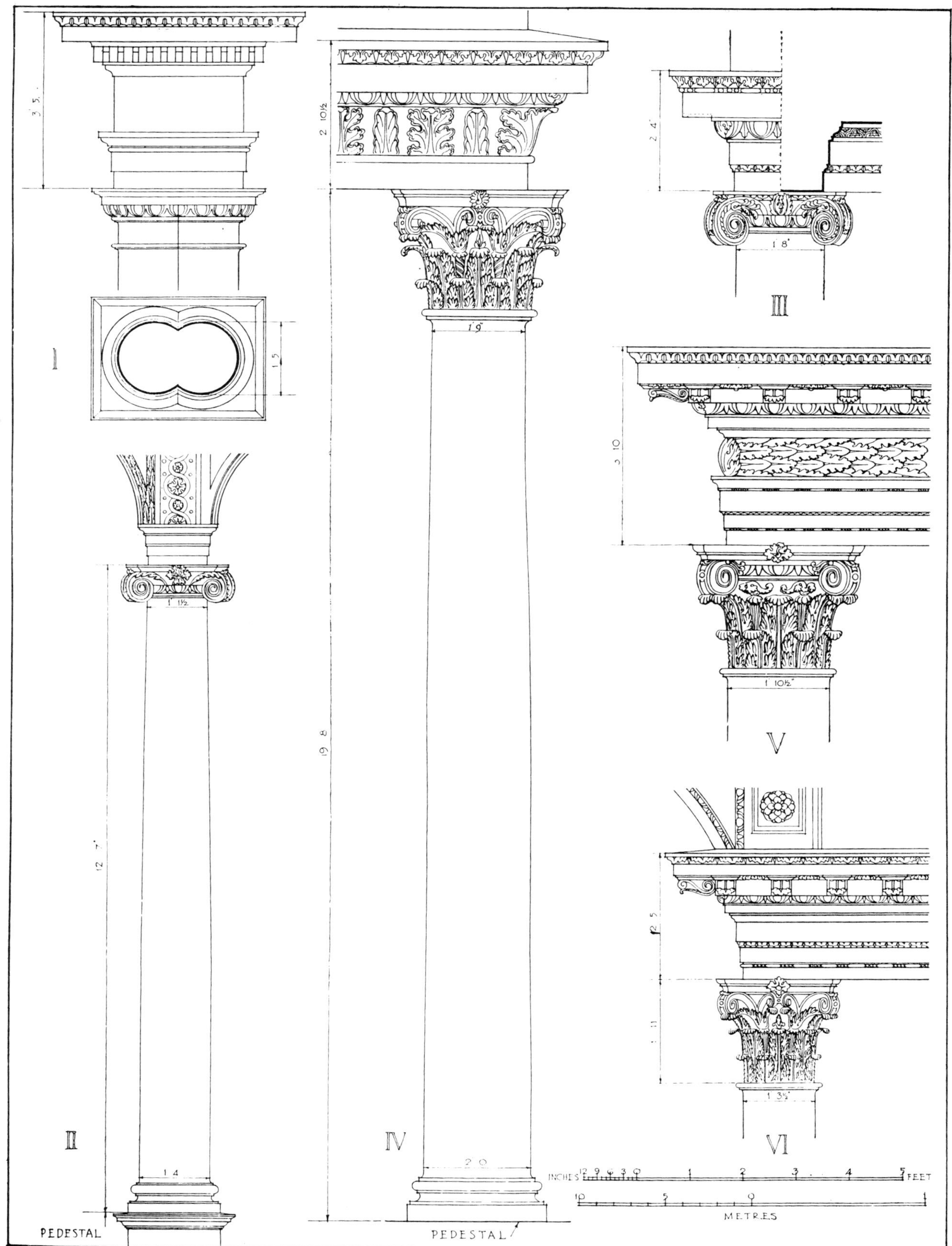

I. Doric Order of Arcades from Church of St Bride, Fleet Street, London.
II. Ionic Order of Nave Columns from Church of St Augustine, Watling Street, London.
III. Ionic Order of Nave Columns from Church of St James, Garlick hythe, London.
IV. Interior Corinthian Order from Church of St Stephen, Walbrook, London.
V. Interior Composite Order from Church of St Martin, Ludgate Hill, London.
VI. Interior Corinthian Order from Church of St Anne and St Agnes, Aldersgate, London.

THE PORTICO OF THE CHURCH OF ST MARTIN-IN-THE-FIELDS, LONDON.

James Gibbs, Architect.

THE PORTICO OF UNIVERSITY COLLEGE, LONDON. *William Wilkins, Architect.*

SOCIETY OF ARTS, JOHN STREET, ADELPHI, LONDON.
FRONT ELEVATION.

HOUSE OF SIR WATKYNS WILLIAMS WYNN, 20 ST JAMES'S SQUARE, LONDON.
ELEVATION OF REAR BLOCK TO COURTYARD.

SION HOUSE, ISLEWORTH, MIDDLESEX.

IONIC ORDER OF THE ANTE-ROOM.

ENTABLATURE OF DOORWAY.

LANSDOWNE HOUSE, FORMERLY SHELBURNE HOUSE, BERKELEY SQUARE, LONDON.

CORINTHIAN ORDER OF THE DINING-ROOM.

THE INCORPORATED LAW SOCIETY'S BUILDING, CHANCERY LANE, LONDON.
CENTRE PART OF FAÇADE.
Designed and Drawn by Lewis Vulliamy, Architect.

THE QUEEN'S HOUSE, GREENWICH, LONDON.
PART OF FAÇADE DESIGNED BY INIGO JONES.
From a Drawing by Lewis Vulliamy.

TRINITY HOUSE, TOWER HILL, LONDON.

PRINCIPAL FAÇADE.

S. Wyatt, Architect.

THE BANK OF ENGLAND, LONDON.

THE LOTHBURY COURTYARD.

From an Aquatint by Thomas Malton.

Sir John Soane, Architect.

VIEW OF WING AT PRESTON HALL, MIDLOTHIAN, AS SEEN FROM WITHIN THE DRAWING-ROOM.

Robert Mitchell, Architect.

GATEWAY AT SOMERSET HOUSE, LONDON.

Sir William Chambers, Architect.

From Aquatints by Thomas Malton.

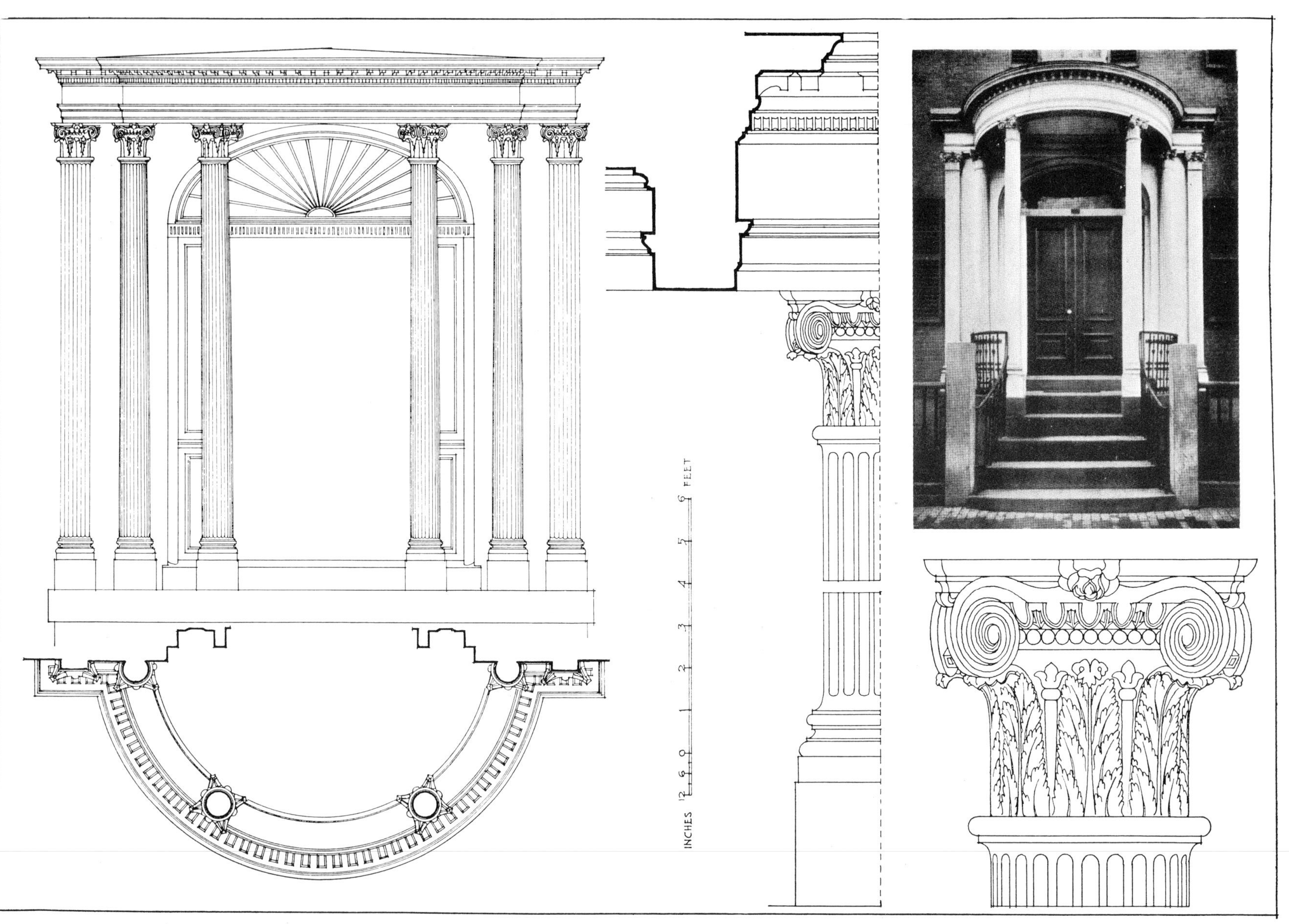

WOOD PORCH AT SALEM, MASSACHUSETTS, U.S.A.

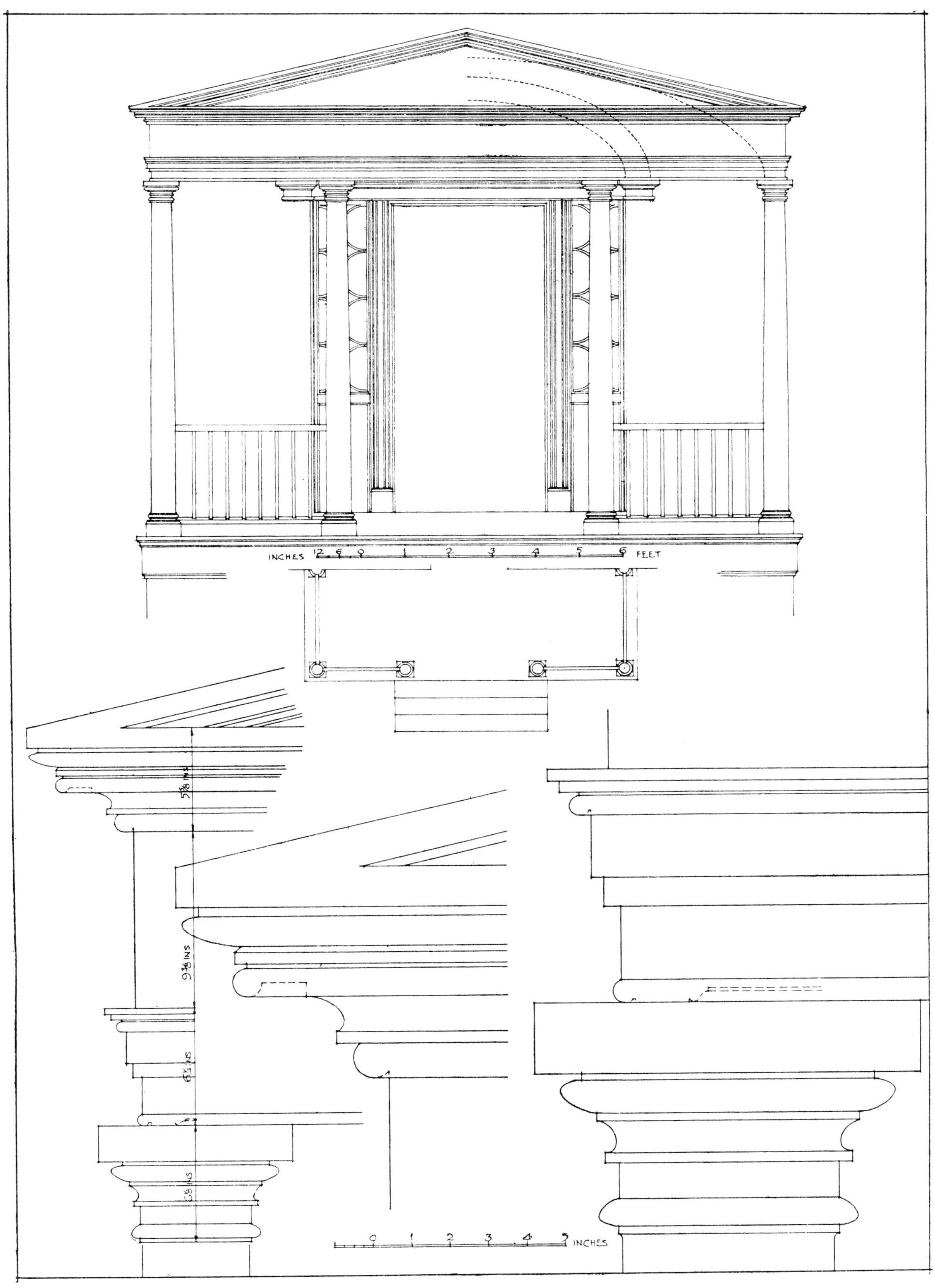

WOOD PORCH, 3123 DUMBARTON AVENUE, COLUMBIA, U.S.A.

THE NORTH DOORWAY OF THE ERECHTHEUM, ATHENS.

ELEVATION AND DETAILS.

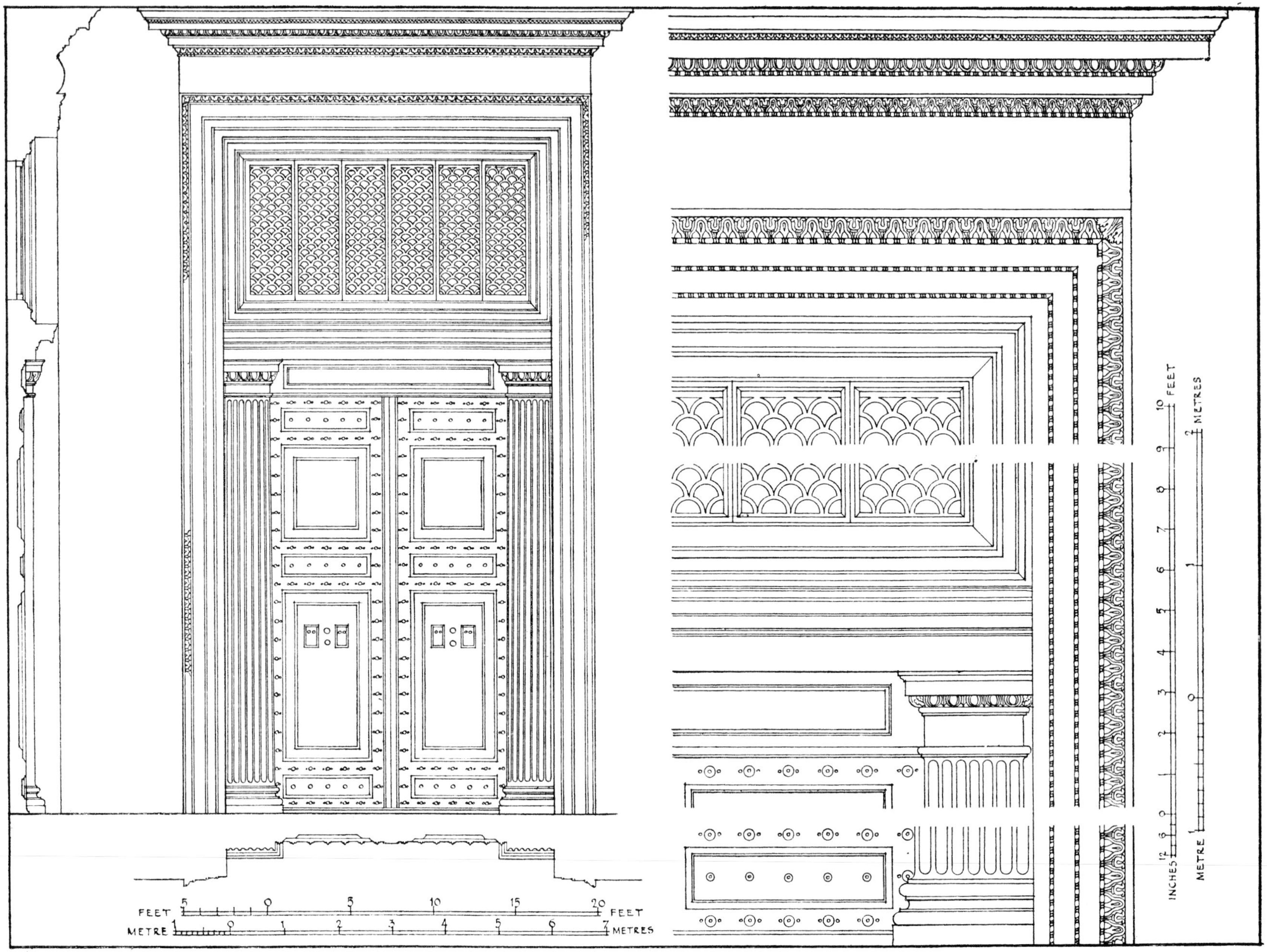

THE PANTHEON, ROME.

Principal Doorway beneath the Portico.

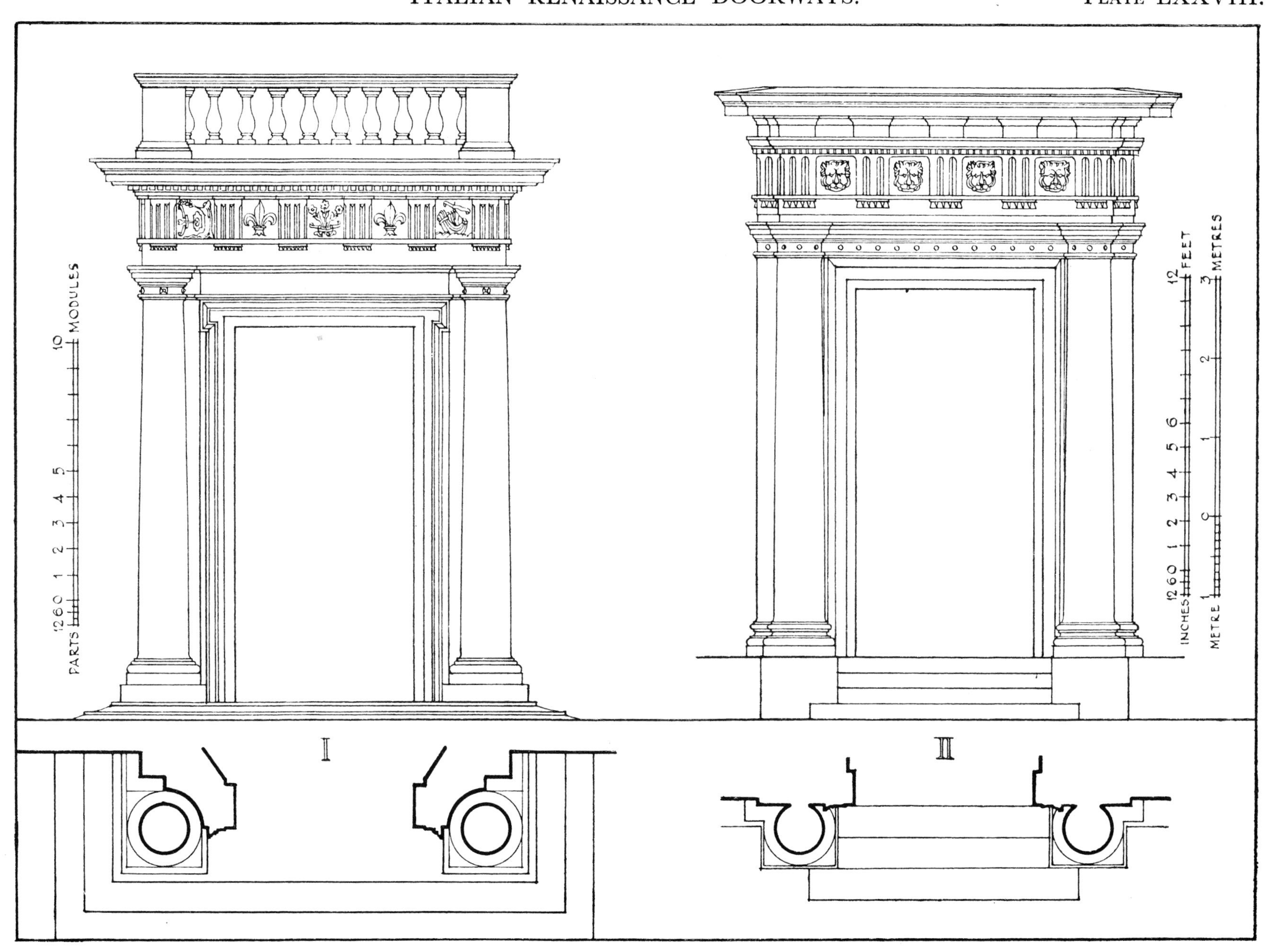

I. THE PALAZZO CANCELLARIA, ROME.
DOORWAY DESIGNED BY VIGNOLA, BUT NOT EXECUTED.

II. THE PALAZZO ALBERGATI, BOLOGNA.
Baldassare Peruzzi, Architect.

ITALIAN RENAISSANCE WINDOWS.

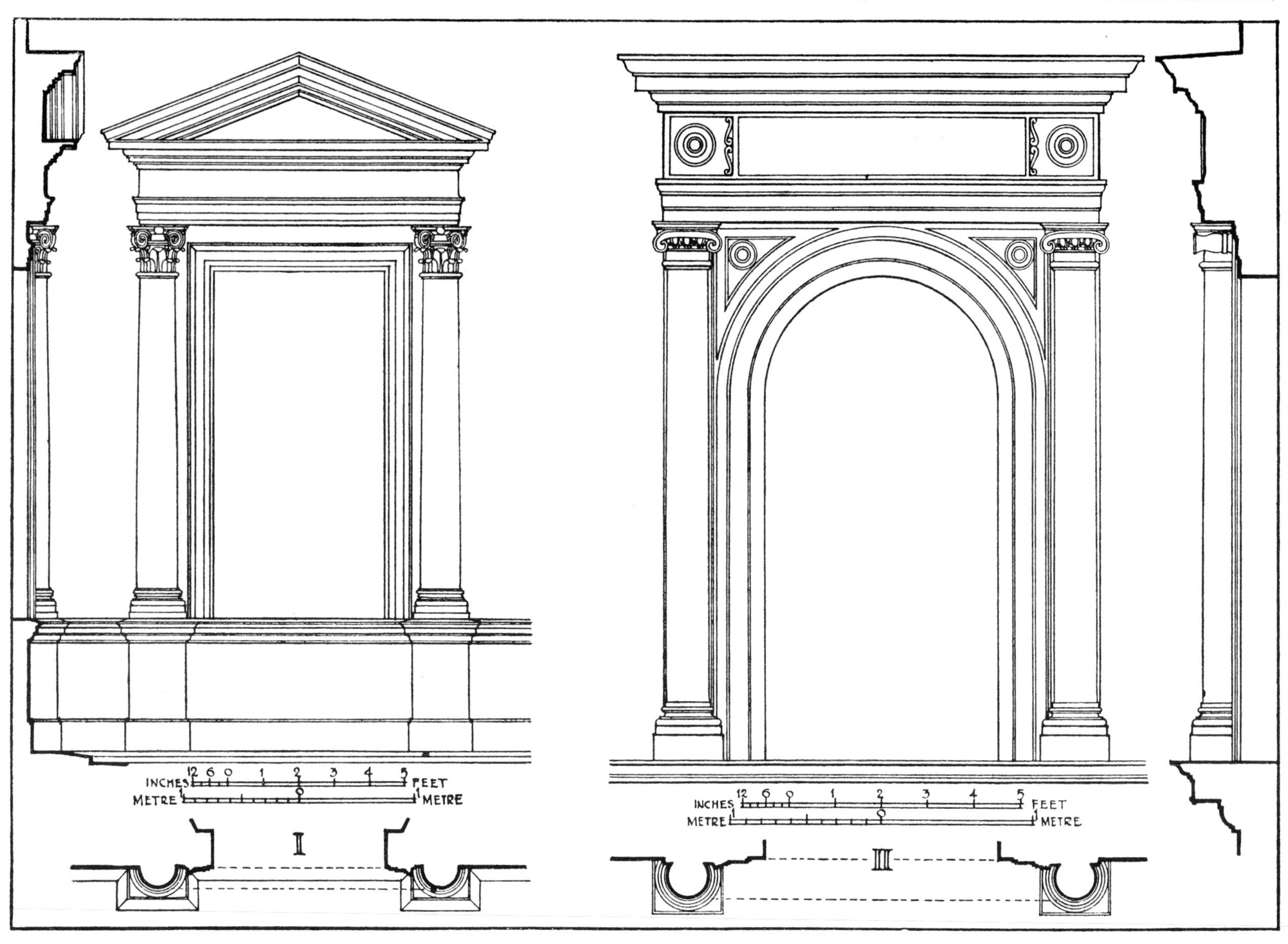

I. THE PALAZZO FARNESE, ROME.

Antonio da San Gallo, Architect.

II. THE PALAZZO ALBERGATI, BOLOGNA.

Baldassare Peruzzi, Architect.

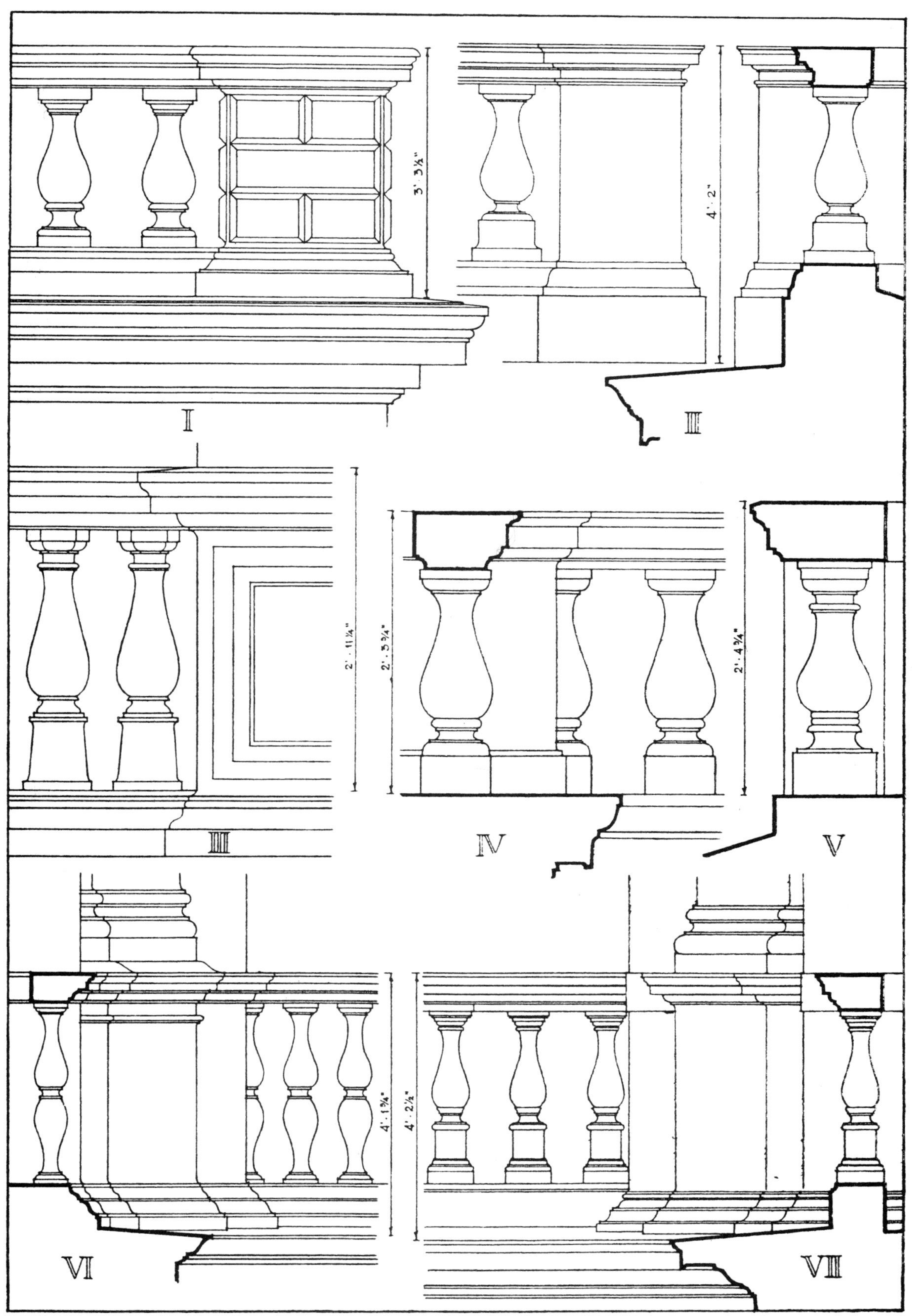

I., II., III. FROM THE "CASTLE" OF CAPRAROLA.
Vignola, Architect.

IV. FROM THE PALAZZO LANTE, ROME.
Baldassare Peruzzi, Architect.

V. FROM THE PALAZZO FARNESE, ROME.
A. da San Gallo, Architect.

VI., VII. FROM THE VATICAN, ROME. CORTILE SAN DAMASO. *Bramante, Architect.*

NOTES ON INTER-COLUMNIATION, SUPERIMPOSITION, AND THE ANTA AND PILASTER.

THE inter-columniation is usually considered to be the distance in the clear between the columns, but it is sometimes taken as the distance from centre to centre of the columns: it is always described in terms of the diameter, or half-diameter, *i.e.*, the module.

The Greek names for the various inter-columniations are found in the writings of Vitruvius. The following are the principal :—

Pycnostyle, in which the columns are placed $1\frac{1}{2}$ diameters or 3 modules apart.

Systyle, 4 modules apart.

Eustyle, $4\frac{1}{2}$ modules apart with a centre inter-columniation of 6 modules.

Diastyle, 6 modules apart.

Areostyle, 7 modules, a wide spacing used with architraves of wood.

Coupled columns are usually placed 1 module apart. Nothing resembling the areosystyle, or a disposition in which the columns are alternately coupled and placed wide apart (Fig. 21), is found in the building of the ancients.

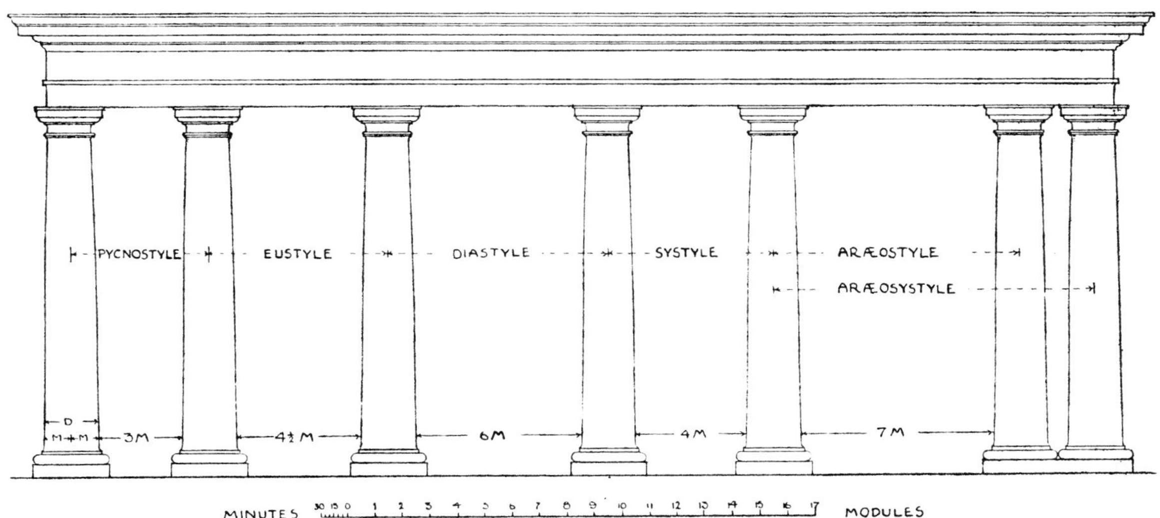

FIG. 21.—DIAGRAM SHOWING THE PRINCIPAL INTER-COLUMNIATIONS.

In no known Greek temples do such exact inter-columniations occur. It was left for the writers of the Renaissance to systematise the Vitruvian spacings and apply them in their work. Thus in the Parthenon, Athens, the general inter-columniation of the peristyle is about $1\frac{1}{5}$ diameters, but in all Greek Doric temples the spacing of the columns is determined by the positions of the triglyphs in the frieze rather than by any regular alternations of solids and voids. The triglyphs are everywhere placed vertically over the axes of the columns, except at the angles, where they are set at the extreme ends of the frieze, and the angle inter-columniations are slightly reduced in order to facilitate this refinement in design.

In the Italian Doric Order the end inter-columniations are the same as the others.

SUPERIMPOSITION OF ORDERS

Fig. 22.—DIAGRAM SHOWING SUPERIMPOSITION OF ORDERS.

Superimposition implies the placing of one Order above another, as was done by the Romans in their amphitheatres, and largely practised during the Renaissance. The simpler and more massive Orders are naturally placed lowermost: thus, Tuscan, when introduced, supports the Doric, the Doric the Ionic, the Ionic the Corinthian or Composite, and the Corinthian the Composite only. In placing columns one above another the axes must always be in the same vertical line when seen in front elevation, but in section it is advisable that the upper ones should be set back, as shown by the dotted axial lines on the diagram (Fig. 22). This readily results from the reduction in the thickness of the wall against which they are set, and from the diminution in the diameter of the upper columns: the slightly pyramidical effect thus obtained helps the composition and prevents the upper storeys from looking top-heavy.

When the same Order is repeated at a higher level it is desirable slightly to diminish the diameter of the upper columns, with an appropriate reduction of the details of the whole Order, since this device obviates any effect of excessive solidity in the upper part of the building. But when different Orders are superimposed this is particularly necessary; otherwise the lower Orders would be overpowered by the upper. A good method is to make the lower diameter of each shaft equal to the upper diameter of the shaft immediately below it. This system makes the intercolumniation in each storey—when expressed in terms of the diameter of the column—six-fifths of that of the storey below.

The cornices should be given rather less projection than when used singly, to prevent their damaging the general proportions by cutting off too much height as seen from below. The topmost entablature, on the other hand, may be slightly increased in all its dimensions in view of its importance as the crowning member of the entire structure. The balustrade—where there is one—must be raised on a plain plinth. The actual height of the storeys themselves may be somewhat modified by the use of continuous plinths and pedestals beneath the columns.

THE rectangular projection at the end of the wing wall of a Greek temple (Figs. 23 and 24) is known as an anta, and its treatment is distinct from that of the columns with which it is used. This is always noticeable in the capital, and when occurring with the Greek Doric Order it is generally further distinguished by the provision of a moulded base. With the Ionic Order, the base is the same for both column and anta, but the anta capital is entirely different, and most Greek examples take a form which allows of small volutes at the angles; but there are many varieties of Ionic anta capital, of which that shown on Plate VII. is an interesting example. Columns standing between antæ are said to be *in antis*, and this term is also used when columns of a Roman or Renaissance Order stand between pilasters (Plate XXVIII.).

FIG. 23.—THE GREEK ANTA IN RELATION TO COLUMNS OF THE GREEK DORIC ORDER.

All such projections occurring with Roman and Renaissance Orders are known as pilasters, and they correspond in the proportions of shaft, capital, and base with the columns of the Order to which they belong. Pilasters are used as responds in conjunction with columns to receive the ends of architraves (Fig. 25, 1), in which case they usually project not less than one-sixth of their width: they are also placed immediately behind columns (Fig. 25, 2 and 3, and Plate XLIX.), then they need not project more than one-eighth of their width, or even less.

Divergent opinions have been

expressed as to the desirability of diminishing pilasters, and in many examples the shafts do not diminish, but when they taper to the same extent as the columns with which they are used, the tendency to appear wider at the top than at the bottom is avoided, and the capital takes a better proportion. The front face is sometimes diminished, leaving the sides vertical. The shafts of pilasters are often fluted, usually with seven flutes on the front face (Fig. 25, 4); an odd number is desirable except in re-entering pilasters, where four flutes are placed instead of three and a half, and five instead of four and a half where the whole pilaster would have nine.

Fig. 24.—PLAN SHOWING THE GREEK ANTA.

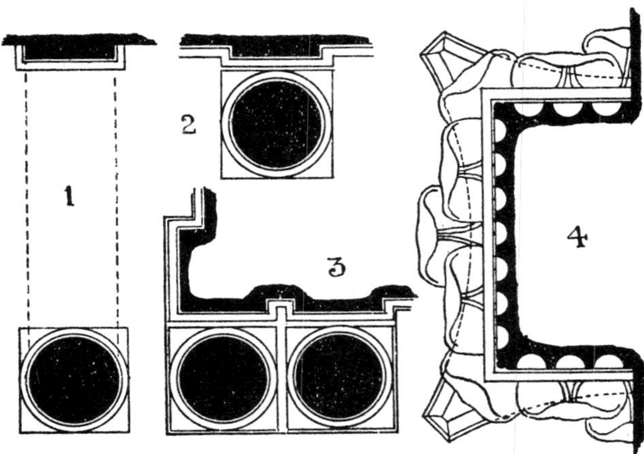

Fig. 25.—THE PILASTER.

1. As a Respond in Conjunction with Column.
2, 3. Immediately Behind Single and Coupled Columns.
4. Plan of a Fluted Corinthian Pilaster, looking up.

Fig. 26.—INTERNAL ORDER FROM A TEMPLE ADJOINING THE BATHS AT NÎMES.

BRIEF GLOSSARY OF TERMS USED IN CONNECTION WITH THE ORDERS OF ARCHITECTURE

ABACUS.—The topmost member of a capital generally square on plan. The sides are concave in the Corinthian and Composite Orders (Plates XLII. and XLVIII.) and curved over the angle volute of the Greek Ionic capital.

ACANTHUS.—A prickly leaved plant, conventionalised by the Greeks, which has afforded a basis for a great variety of carved ornament in Classic and Renaissance buildings (Fig. 8 and Plate XXIV. I.).

ACROTERIUM (*pl.* ACROTERIA).—The blocks at the angles or apex of a pediment to carry sculptures or ornaments.

AGORA.—The public square or market-place in a Greek city corresponding to the forum in a Roman city.

AMPHI-PROSTYLE.—The term applied to a temple with free standing columns in the front and rear only.

ANCONES.—(1) The vertical brackets on either side of a Greek (Plate LXXVI.) or Roman (Fig. 20) doorway supporting the cornice over the same. (2) Projecting bosses left on masonry blocks.

ANNULET.—Any one of the small horizontal channels, circular on plan, below the echinus of the Greek Doric capital (Plate IV.).

ANTA (*pl.* ANTÆ). *See* pages 41 and 42, and Figs. 23, 24.

ANTEFIX (*pl.* ANTEFIXA).—The decorative termination of the roof tile or tile-roll of a roof placed above the cornice, especially along the sides of a Greek Doric temple (Plate IV.).

ANTHEMION.—The term given to the sheathing leaves of the flower of the acanthus often, but wrongly, called honeysuckle (Fr. *palmette*). It is used in various ways to decorate acroteria, antefixa, friezes (Plate XIII.), and the necking of some Ionic capitals (Plate VII.).

APOPHYGE.—The cavetto or concave sweep taken by the end of the shaft of a column in its junction with the upper or lower fillet.

ARCHITRAVE.—(1) A lintel carried from the top of one column to another or from the top of an anta (Fig. 23) pilaster or pier to an adjacent supporting member. (2) The lowest member of the Classic entablature in all Orders. (3) The term is also applied to a moulded member carried round the sides and head of an opening, niche, etc. (Plate LXXVIII.).

ARCHIVOLT.—A moulded architrave (def. 3 above) carried round an arch in any position (Plates XXXI. and XXXII.).

AREOSTYLE.—Inter-columniation. *See* page 39 and Fig. 21.

AREOSYSTYLE.—Inter-columniation. *See* page 39 and Fig. 21.

ASTRAGAL (literally, a knuckle-bone).—A small convex moulding, when plain more often called a bead, and often carved with bead-and-reel enrichment (Plate XIII.).

ATTIC.—The term applied to a storey above the main cornice, whether, as in the case of a Roman triumphal arch, decorated with bas-reliefs or utilized for an inscription (Plate XXIII.), or forming an additional storey as in the Palazzo Valmarana, Vicenza (Plate LIV.) and many Renaissance façades.

ATTIC BASE.—The standard base of the Romans, consisting primarily of an upper and lower torus separated by a scotia (Plate XVI.).

BANDED ORDER.—In Renaissance buildings certain Orders with columns formed of circular blocks alternately projecting are said to be banded (Plate LXIII.).

BASE.—The lowermost division of a column, anta, or pilaster, usually moulded. By spreading beyond the line of the vertical shaft it affords a larger bearing surface for the distribution of the load supported and produces an effect of greater stability. The columns of all Orders have bases, with the exception of the Greek Doric Order. *See* page 6.

CAULICOLUS.—The stalk of the acanthus plant as conventionalised in the Greek stele and in the various renderings of the capital of the Corinthian and Composite Orders.

CELLA.—The enclosed chamber or sanctuary of a Roman temple corresponding to the naos of the Greek temple.

COFFER.—A sunk panel in the surface of a vault, dome, or soffit of an arch in Roman buildings and in similar and additional positions in Renaissance buildings. The sunk panels in a Greek ceiling are known as lacunaria.

COLONNADE.—A range of columns supporting a horizontal entablature (Plate V.), as distinct from an arcade, which is a range of columns or piers supporting arches (Plate LX.).

CORNICE.—The uppermost of the three principal divisions of a Classic or Renaissance entablature : it is subdivided into bed-mould, corona, and cymatium. Projecting members, provided to accentuate horizontal divisions and at the same time to throw rainwater away from the face of a wall, are also known as cornices, and are of frequent occurrence in Renaissance façades.

CORONA.—The centre member of a Classic cornice projecting above the bed-mould and usually with a vertical face and uncarved.

CYMA.—A moulding of double curvature. When the concave portion is uppermost it is called a cyma recta : when the convex part is at the top it is called a cyma reversa.

CYMATIUM.—The crowning moulding of an entablature when it takes the cyma recta form.

DADO.—The lower portion of a wall when treated as a separate architectural feature.

DENTIL.—One of a number of small blocks spaced near together and forming a dentil band, introduced just above the bed-mould of the Greek Ionic cornice (Plate VI.), and in a similar position in the cornices of the Roman Orders (Plates XIV. and XVI.), and in the cornices of all the Italian Orders, except the Tuscan.

DIASTYLE.—Inter-columniation. *See* page 39 and Fig. 21.

DIE.—(1) The square base of a column. (2) The vertical face of a pedestal or podium between the cornice and base of a pedestal (Plate XXVI.).

DIPTERAL.—Term applied to a temple surrounded by two rows of columns : a double peristyle.

DISTYLE-IN-ANTIS.—A disposition of two columns between antæ or pilasters, as in the porticoes of small buildings of both ancient and Renaissance times (Plate XXVIII.). A temple may be distyle-in-antis at one or both ends (amphi-distyle-in-antis), but the disposition precludes a peripteral arrangement.

ECHINUS.—In the capital of the Greek Doric Order the convex member, circular on plan, immediately beneath the abacus, which it supports (Plate IV.).

It occurs also between and beneath the volutes of the Ionic capital (Plates VIII. and XXXVIII.). It was generally painted with the Doric Order and carved with the Ionic Order.

ENTABLATURE.—The trabeation carried by columns. It is divided into three parts: (*a*) the architrave, (*b*) the frieze, and (*c*) the cornice. In Renaissance buildings it is often "returned" round pilasters and columns, both attached and detached (Plate XLIX.), and on façades, it often completes the upper part of a wall even when there is no Order. A slice of entablature is sometimes introduced between the capital of a detached column and the springing of the arch it supports (Fig. 15), but this is preferably omitted in most situations unless a modified form of entablature is introduced (Fig. 11).

ENTASIS.—The graceful profile of the shaft of a column. It is the slightly convex curve given to the shaft in order to correct an optical illusion which causes a shaft bounded by absolutely straight lines to appear hollow or concave at its mid-height. For methods of setting out, *see* Plate XLIV. and page 33.

EPISTYLE.—The Greek term for the architrave.

EUSTYLE.—Inter-columniation. *See* page 39 and Fig. 21.

FASCIA.—The term given to the planes into which the architrave is divided in the ancient and Renaissance Orders.

FILLET.—A small flat member of rectangular section occurring in a variety of positions, but usually separating mouldings. A fillet always occurs above the cyma of a cornice.

FLUTES.—The vertical channels with which the shafts of columns are generally cut. They may be semi-circular, segmental, or elliptical in true section, separated from one another by arrises in the Doric Orders and by fillets in the other Orders. In some Roman and Renaissance Ionic and Corinthian Orders the lower portion of the flute up to about one-third of the height of the shaft was filled in with a convex moulding to which the term "cabling" is applied (Plate LXIV.). Late Roman and Renaissance Orders sometimes present examples of fluting carried spirally round the shafts (Plate LVIII.).

FRIEZE.—(1) The middle member of the entablature. (2) Any horizontal band enriched with sculpture or decorative ornament.

GUILLOCHE.—A convex moulding carved with interwoven fillets leaving circular centres (Plate XIII. v.). Similar interwoven patterns are sometimes carved on flat bands.

GUTTÆ (Drops).—Small pendant members beneath the mutules and triglyphs of any Doric entablature (Plates IV. and XXXIII.).

HELIX.—The spiral tendril beneath the abacus of the Corinthian capital. There are 16 helices in perfect examples, 2 at each angle and 2 beneath the centre of each concave side of the abacus (Plates XXI. and XLII.).

HEXASTYLE.—A portico having six columns in front (Plates V. and XIX.).

IMPOST.—The member, usually moulded, which marks the springing of an arch (Plates XIV. and LII.).

INTER-COLUMNIATION.—The distance between the columns of an Order, always defined in terms of the lower diameter of the column. *See* page 39 and Fig. 21.

KEYSTONE.—The central stone of a semicircular arch, often sculptured or carved (Plates XXIII. and XL.).

METOPE.—The space between the triglyphs in the frieze of the Doric Order, approximately square and generally filled with sculptured or carved slabs (Plates IV. and XXX.). In the Doric Order as used by the Renaissance masters a half-metope occurs at every angle owing to the literal spacing of the angle triglyph over the axis of the column (Plate XXX.). This weak arrangement is avoided in the Greek Doric Order (Plates III.-V.).

MODILLION.—The horizontal brackets or corbels beneath the projecting corona of the Corinthian and Composite Orders (Plates XX.-XXII.). They are placed vertically on a sloping cornice (Plate XLIII.).

MODULE.—The half-diameter of the lower part of the shaft of a column. *See* page viii.

MONOLITH COLUMN.—One formed of a single block as regards the total height of the shaft.

MUTULE.—The slab upon the soffit of the corona of the Doric cornice, occurring over each triglyph and over each metope (Plates IV. and XXIII.). It is usually the same width as the triglyph, and from its soffit hang rows of guttæ.

NAOS.—The term given to the cella of a Greek temple.

NECKING.—The space between the astragal at the top of the shaft of a column and the lowest member of the capital itself especially in the Roman and Renaissance Doric Orders (Plates XV. and XXXII.).

OCTASTYLE.—A portico having eight columns in front.

PEDIMENT.—In Classic architecture the triangular termination of a roof, bounded by horizontal and sloping cornices (pages 31, 33) and containing a wall space which, whether plain or sculptured, is known as a tympanum (Plate XIX.). In Renaissance buildings, any roof end whether triangular, curved, or broken (Fig. 15).

PERIPTERAL.—A building entirely surrounded by isolated columns, such as the Parthenon, Athens, is said to be peripteral: when the columns, or some of them, are attached, as in the Maison Carrée, Nîmes (Plate XIX.), the building is said to be pseudo-peripteral.

PERISTYLE.—(1) A covered colonnade surrounding a building or court. (2) The inner court of a Roman or Pompeian house.

PLINTH.—The lowest square member of the base of a column.

PODIUM.—The low wall or continuous pedestal on which columns are carried. It consists of a die with cornice and base, and most Roman temples were raised in this manner (Fig. 7), while the podium is of frequent occurrence in Renaissance buildings (Plate LXVII.).

PORTICO.—An arrangement of columns supporting an entablature and usually a pediment, forming a frontispiece to most classic temples (Plate V. and Fig. 7), and a dignified entrance to many Renaissance buildings (Plates LXVI. and LXVII.). A portico having two columns in front between antæ or pilasters is known as distyle-in-antis (Plates VI. and XXVIII.); with four columns in front, tetrastyle prostyle (Plate XXIX.); with six columns in front, hexastyle (Plate V.); with eight columns, octastyle; with ten columns, decastyle (Plate LXVII.); and with twelve columns, dodecastyle.

PRONAOS.—The porticoed space in front of the naos.

PROPYLÆUM.—The entrance to the sacred enclosure of a Greek temple when there is one doorway only; when there is more than one doorway, as in the entrance to the Acropolis at Athens, the plural term "propylæa" is used (Fig. 1).

PROSTYLE.—The term applied to a temple with a portico of columns standing clear in front (Plate I.).

PSEUDO-DIPTERAL.—The term applied to a dipteral temple with the inner row of columns omitted.

PSEUDO-PERIPTERAL.—Term applied to a peripteral temple where some of the columns are engaged in the walls of the cella, as in many Roman temples (Plate XIX.).

PULVIN.—(1) The "cushion" or "bolster" sides of an Ionic capital. (2) A frieze of convex section is known as a pulvinated frieze (Plate LXV. v.).

PYCNOSTYLE.—Inter-columniation. *See* page 39 and Fig. 21.

Regula.—A narrow rectangular member beneath the tænia of the Doric architrave below which guttæ are carved.

Respond.—(1) The wall pilaster behind a column (Fig. 25). (2) The wall pier carrying either the end of an architrave or the springing of an arch.

Rustication.—Masonry with roughened surfaces and recessed joints extensively used in Renaissance times as a means of obtaining the desired expression (Plates L. and LXIII.). Renaissance Orders with projecting square blocks in the shafts of the columns or pilasters are said to be rusticated (Plates LXIII. and LXXIII.).

Shaft.—That part of a Classic column between the capital and the base.

Stoa.—In a Greek city a term for the structure corresponding to the Roman porticus.

Stylobate.—The upper step of a peripteral temple which forms a platform for the columns. In a Greek Doric temple the term is usually applied to all the steps, generally three in number (Plates I. and III.).

Superimposition of Orders.—*See* page 39 and Fig. 21.

Systyle.—Inter-columniation. *See* page 39 and Fig. 21.

Tænia.—The projecting fillet which crowns the architrave of the Doric entablature in both ancient and Renaissance Orders.

Tetrastyle.—A portico having four columns in front (Plate XXIX.).

Torus.—A convex moulding, larger than a bead, and of frequent occurrence in Classic base mouldings when it is enriched with guilloche and other carved ornament (Plates VII. and XIII. v.).

Triglyphs.—Blocks peculiar to the Doric frieze, with vertical V-shaped channels cut in their faces (Plate IV.). Two complete channels and two half-channels make the three *glyphs* or channels from which the triglyph obtains its name.

Tympanum.—The triangular space between the horizontal and sloping cornices on the front of a pediment (Plates XIX. and LXVI.).

Volute (Lat., **Voluta**, a scroll).—The scroll or spiral occurring in Ionic, Corinthian, and Composite capitals. For method of setting out, *see* Plate XXXVIII. and page 32.

Voussoir.—A wedge-shaped stone forming one of the units of a masonry arch.

Wreathed Shaft.—The shaft of a column when twisted, as shown on Plate XLIV. iii. iv., it can be readily set out according to the method shown on that Plate and explained on page 34. Baroque architecture affords instances of the use of this form of shaft which are more ingenious than logical.

Fig. 27. CAPITAL FROM A TEMPLE ADJOINING THE BATHS AT NÎMES.

INDEX TO TEXT AND ILLUSTRATIONS

The large numerals, thus XXVI., *refer to plate numbers. The small numerals, thus* IV., *indicate the particular subjects on the plate referred to. The illustrations referred to thus,* Fig. 8, *will be found in the text*